S0-AFF-318

LE CORDON BLEU

CLASSIC LIGHT

LE CORDON BLEU

CLASSIC LIGHT

Sophisticated food for healthy living

JENI WRIGHT AND
LE CORDON BLEU CHEFS

CASSELL&CO

First published in the United Kingdom in 2000
by Cassell & Co

Text copyright © 2000 LE CORDON BLEU
LIMITED
Design and layout copyright © Cassell & Co 2000

The moral right of LE CORDON BLEU
LIMITED to be identified as the author of this
work has been asserted in accordance with the
Copyright, Designs and Patents Act of 1988

All rights reserved. No part of this publication may
be reproduced in any material form (including
photocopying or storing it in any medium by
electronic means and whether or not transiently or
incidentally to some other use of this publication)
without the written permission of the copyright
owner, except in accordance with the provisions of
the Copyright, Designs and Patents Act 1988 or
under the terms of a licence issued by the
Copyright Licensing Agency, 90 Tottenham Court
Road, London W1P 9HE. Applications for the
copyright owner's written permission to reproduce
any part of this publication should be addressed to
the publisher.

Distributed in the United States of America by
Sterling Publishing Co., Inc., 387 Park Avenue
South, New York, NY 10016–8810.

A CIP catalogue record for this book is available
from the British Library

ISBN 0–304–35587–9

Colour separation by Tenon & Polert Colour
Scanning Ltd.

Printed and bound by South China Printing Co.
Ltd, Hong Kong

Designed by Helen James
Photographs by Amanda Heywood
Home Economist Carole Handslip

Cassell & Co
Wellington House
125 Strand
London WC2R 0BB

Le Cordon Bleu and the publishers would like to
express their gratitude to the 42 Masterchefs of all
the Le Cordon Bleu Schools, whose knowledge
and expertise have made this book possible,
especially: Chef Terrien, Chef Boucheret, Chef
Deguignet, Chef Duchêne (MOF), Chef Guillut,
Chef Pinaud, Chef Cros, Paris; Chef Males, Chef
Walsh, Chef Power, Chef Carr, Chef Paton, Chef
Poole-Gleed, Chef Wavrin, Chef Thivet, London;
Chef Chantefort, Chef Jambert, Chef Hamasaki,
Chef Honda, Chef Paucod, Chef Okuda, Chef
Lederf, Chef Peugeot, Chef Mori, Tokyo; Chef
Salambien, Chef Boutin, Chef Harris, Sydney;
Chef Lawes, Adelaide; Chef Guiet, Chef Denis,
Chef Petibon, Chef Poncet, Ottawa; Chef Martin,
Mexico; Chef Camargo, Brazil.

A very special acknowledgement to Helen
Barnard, Alison Oakervee and Deepika Sukhwani
who have been responsible for the co-ordination
of the Le Cordon Bleu team throughout this book
under the Presidency of André Cointreau.

Le Cordon Bleu Schools Worldwide

Paris
8 rue Léon Delhomme, Paris 75015, France
Phone: 33/1 53 68 22 50
Fax: 33/1 48 56 03 96
E-mail: infoparis@cordonbleu.net

London
114 Marylebone Lane, London W1M 6HH, Great Britain
Phone: 44/0 207 935 3503
Toll Free in Great Britain: 0/800 980 3503
Fax: 44/0 207 935 7621
E-mail: london@cordonbleu.net

Tokyo
Roob 1, 28-113 Saragaku-cho, Daikanyama, Shibuya-ku,
Tokyo 150, Japan
Phone: 81/3 54 89 01 41
Fax: 81/3 54 89 01 45
E-mail: tokyoinfo@cordonbleu.net

Ottawa
Suite 400, 1390 Prince of Wales Drive, Ottawa, Ontario
K2C 3N6, Canada
Phone: 1/613 224 8603
Fax: 1/613 224 9966
E-mail: ottawa@cordonbleu.net

Le Cordon Bleu Restaurant, Business and Management -
Adelaide
Regency Campus, 163 Days Road, Regency Park, Adelaide
SA 5010, Australia
Phone: 61/8 8348 4425
Fax: 61/8 8348 4490
E-mail: regency.international@regency.tafe.sa.edu.au

New York Corporate Office
404 Airport Executive Park, Nanuet, New York NY10954
USA
Phone: 1/914 426 7400
Toll Free in the US and Canada: 1/800 457 CHEF
Fax: 1/914 426 0104
E-mail: lcbinfo@cordonbleu.net
Website: http://www.cordonbleu.net

CONTENTS

FOREWORD

Welcome to *Le Cordon Bleu Classic Light*, a fabulous collection of delicious and imaginative dishes that are healthy – and light. The emphasis is on natural fresh ingredients that are good for you. Recipes are based on French cooking techniques and have a wide range of culinary influences, producing an imaginative marriage of flavors without the cream and butter that are normally associated with classic cuisine. Here you will find inspiring, delicious meals that can be eaten every day, either after work or when entertaining at the weekend.

Founded in Paris in 1895, today Le Cordon Bleu has expanded to include 13 schools, restaurants and hospitality management programmes, establishing academic alliances and partnerships as well as an extensive culinary product line. Over four continents, in France, Great Britain, Canada, Japan, Australia, America, Brazil and Mexico, Le Cordon Bleu's Masterchefs share their knowledge with students from 50 countries. They also maintain close links with the culinary industry through attending and participating in over thirty culinary festivals per year.

Le Cordon Bleu's 42 Masterchefs teach classic French techniques in the arena of world cuisine and pâtisserie, inspiring students to appreciate and develop their skills and potentials. Le Cordon Bleu is dedicated to promoting the advancement of education, training and the appreciation of gastronomy worldwide.

The worldwide reputation of Le Cordon Bleu was proven in 1996 when the school was chosen by the Shanghai Tourist Authority to train the first Chinese chefs sent abroad to learn western culinary techniques. In 1997, Le Cordon Bleu opened its fifth school in Sydney, leading to a joint venture with the Australian government to train and advise the chefs for the 2000

Olympic games. Recent developments in Le Cordon Bleu's curriculum have led to the establishment of the bachelor degree in restaurant management, a fast-track intensive qualification for future restaurant professionals and the perfect complement to those skills learned on the renowned Grand Diplôme courses at Le Cordon Bleu.

Motivated students are drawn to Le Cordon Bleu from all walks of life. Those with either professional aspirations or a keen interest in fine cooking benefit immensely from a Le Cordon Bleu education. The name evokes images of quality, tradition, and unerring commitment to excellence at every level. This is increasingly true as Le Cordon Bleu enters its second century and recognizes a modern world of ever-changing lifestyles. Through its courses, consultancy, publications, bistros, bakeries and restaurants, gourmet and licensed products, Le Cordon Bleu is promoting the art of fine living and fine cooking worldwide.

Le Cordon Bleu Classic Light brings the expertise of its chefs into your kitchen. The recipes are simple and delicious, prepared with minimal fuss and effort. Healthy cooking methods and low-fat ingredients are used whenever possible, opening the door for you to continue to discover even more creative possibilities.

Bon Appétit

André J Cointreau
President
Le Cordon Bleu-L'Art Culinaire

SOUPS & STARTERS

Whether you are cooking light or not, it is always sensible
to start a meal with a soup or first course that is light rather than
heavy. Everyone is hungry at the beginning of a meal, so if you
offer large portions of rich or heavy food, everyone is tempted
to eat too much without thinking of what is to follow. The same
goes for spicy foods or ingredients with powerful flavors. These can
leave a lingering taste and spoil the dishes to come. The first rule is
to keep portions small and flavors delicate.

Some of the soups in this chapter are served chilled, which is most
refreshing for summer, but they can be heated through and served
hot in the winter months. Cream, so often used to enrich soups
and garnish starters at the last minute, is not used here, and it is
unlikely you will notice its absence. Instead of cream, you can use
low-fat crème fraîche or plain yogurt to equally good effect, and
there is nothing more eye-catching or appealing than a sprinkling
of chopped fresh herbs or a single stem artfully arranged.

The Orient plays a large part in light cooking. Low-cholesterol and
low-fat ingredients with fragrant aromas and subtle spicing are
hallmarks of most eastern cuisines. When east meets west, as it does
in many of the recipes in this chapter, the collaboration is exquisite.

GAZPACHO

Naturally very low in fat and high in fiber, vitamins, and minerals, this exquisite Spanish soup is a must for the summer months when tomatoes and bell peppers are ripe and full of flavor. For maximum visual impact, serve it in white bowls or a white serving dish.

1 mild Spanish onion

1 cucumber

1 lb ripe tomatoes

3 garlic cloves

1 large red bell pepper

1½ cups fresh white breadcrumbs

1 cup tomato juice

3 tablespoons sherry vinegar

1 teaspoon caster sugar, or to taste

salt and freshly ground black pepper

To Serve

a little extra virgin olive oil

1 handful of shredded fresh basil leaves

Serves 6–8

Preparation time: 20 minutes, plus chilling time

Chef's Tips

The peel of the cucumber gives the soup extra texture, but you can remove it before chopping the cucumber if you like. Sherry vinegar comes from Jerez in Spain, and you can buy bottles of it in most supermarkets. Its flavor is quite musky, which is good in a strong-flavored soup like gazpacho. You can use sherry instead, or a red wine vinegar.

◆

You may have to purée the soup in batches, depending on the size of your machine. This recipe makes about 7½ cups of liquid.

1   Roughly chop the onion, cucumber, tomatoes, and garlic. Quarter, core, and deseed the red bell pepper.

2   Place all of these ingredients in a food processor or blender and add the tomato juice, sherry vinegar, 2½ cups cold water, and sugar, salt and pepper to taste. Purée until the soup is mostly smooth, but retaining a little texture.

3   Pour the soup into a bowl and check the seasoning. Cover and chill in the refrigerator overnight. This will develop the flavors.

To Serve   Stir the soup well and add a little cold water if the consistency is too thick. Taste for seasoning. Ladle into chilled bowls or a serving dish and grind black pepper liberally over the surface. Swirl a little olive oil in the center of the soup and garnish with shredded basil. Serve well chilled.

CRAB AND GINGER WONTON SOUP

Pretty as a picture, this delicate soup is very low in fat and yet full of flavor. In China, wonton soups are served as a snack rather than a first course, but you may prefer to serve this soup for a lunch or supper.

1 small leek	*Wontons*
2 carrots	2 tablespoons pickled ginger
4 fresh cilantro sprigs	1 egg white
1 star anise	brown and white meat from 1 crab
4 tablespoons rice wine	¾ cup fresh white breadcrumbs
salt and freshly ground black pepper	20 round wonton wrappers

Serves 4

Preparation time: 30 minutes
Cooking time: 25 minutes

1   Make the broth. Roughly chop and wash the green part of the leek and place in a large saucepan. Cut the white part into fine julienne strips, wash and set aside. Roughly chop 1 carrot and add to the pan. Cut the remaining carrot into julienne strips and set aside.

2   Strip the leaves from the cilantro and set aside. Add the stalks to the pan with the star anise, rice wine, 4 cups cold water, and salt and pepper to taste. Bring to a boil and simmer for 10 minutes, then cover and remove from the heat.

3   Make the wontons. Finely chop the ginger. Beat the egg white in a bowl until frothy, then transfer 2 teaspoons to a saucer. Mix the crab, ginger, and breadcrumbs into the egg white in the bowl; season well. Place a little mixture in the center of each wrapper. Brush a little reserved egg white around the edges of the wrappers, then gather them around the filling like little bags. Twist just above the filling to seal tightly and expel any trapped air.

4   Strain the stock into a clean saucepan and discard the flavorings. Taste for seasoning, then bring to a simmer. Add the wontons and poach for 2 minutes. Add the carrot and poach for another minute, then add the leek and poach for a further 2 minutes.

To Serve   Divide the wontons equally between 4 warm soup bowls and ladle in the broth. Sprinkle with the reserved cilantro leaves and serve immediately.

Chef's Tips

Rice wine is made from fermented rice. It is used in Chinese cooking for its rich, mellow flavor and golden color, and it is also served as a drink. The best kind is Shaoxing, which you will find in Chinese shops, but you can buy other good brands at most supermarkets. Dry or medium dry sherry can also be used instead; don't use the Japanese rice wine called sake, which is colorless.

◆

Wonton wrappers are made from wheat flour, egg, and water. They come in both round and square shapes, and are yellow in color. For this recipe you need round wontons, about 3 inches in diameter. You can get them in oriental shops.

VICHYSSOISE

Classic vichyssoise is made with lots of butter and cream. This version only has a small amount of butter and no cream. It tastes so good you will hardly notice the difference. In fact, you will probably prefer it to its rich predecessor.

2 tablespoons butter

4 cups sliced leeks

1¼ cups finely chopped onion

1⅔ cups diced potatoes

about 3½ cups chicken or vegetable stock

pinch of freshly grated nutmeg

salt and freshly ground black pepper

To Serve

4 tablespoons low-fat plain yogurt

1 tablespoon chopped fresh chives

Serves 4

Preparation time: 20 minutes, plus cooling and chilling time
Cooking time: 40 minutes

Chef's Tip

Keep some stock in the refrigerator while chilling the soup in case you need some for thinning the soup down before serving.

◆

Variation

Serve the soup hot: after puréeing, return it to the rinsed pan and reheat until bubbling, stirring frequently. Add more stock if the consistency is too thick and stir until combined and heated through, then taste for seasoning.

1　Melt the butter in a large saucepan, add the leeks and onion and stir to mix with the butter. Cover the pan and sweat the vegetables over low heat for 5–7 minutes until soft but not colored. Stir them occasionally and take care not to let them brown.

2　Add the potatoes and stock. Bring to a boil, cover, and simmer for about 30 minutes or until the potatoes are very soft. Season with the nutmeg, and salt and pepper to taste.

3　Pour the soup into a food processor or blender and purée until smooth. Pour into a bowl and leave to cool, then cover and chill in the refrigerator for at least 4 hours, preferably overnight.

To Serve　Stir the soup well and add a little more chilled stock if the consistency is too thick. Taste for seasoning. Ladle into chilled bowls and top with a spoonful of yogurt and a sprinkling of chives. Serve well chilled.

SUMMER MINESTRONE

We tend to think of minestrone as a strongly flavored red soup thick with tomatoes, beans, and pasta, but there are many different types of minestrone in Italy. This one is delicate, fresh, and green with new season's vegetables and herbs.

1 onion
1 celery stick
1 garlic clove
3 ½ oz fine green beans
1 medium zucchini
1 tablespoon olive oil
salt and freshly ground black pepper
5 cups vegetable or chicken stock
¾ cup shelled fresh garden peas
1 cup cooked white rice
2 tablespoons chopped soft fresh herbs (eg chervil, tarragon, parsley, basil)
shavings of Parmesan cheese, to serve

Serves 4–6

Preparation time: 15 minutes
Cooking time: 30–35 minutes

Chef's Tips

For authenticity, use a short-grain arborio or other risotto rice. To get 1 cup of cooked rice, you will need ⅓ cup uncooked rice.

◆

If you like you can dice the vegetables in a food processor, but take care not to overprocess them to a mush. If you have time, it is better to dice the vegetables with a sharp knife for this recipe. The finished soup will look more attractive if the vegetables are diced to a neat, uniform shape.

◆

Variation

Use a small soup pasta (pastina) instead of rice. If you go to an Italian delicatessen you will find many different and unusual shapes to choose from. There is even a tiny shape called risoni, which looks like grains of rice. Use the same quantity of pasta as rice.

1 Finely dice the onion and celery. Crush the garlic. Cut the beans crosswise into 1 inch pieces and cut the zucchini into small, even-sized chunks.

2 Heat the oil in a large saucepan and sweat the onion, celery, and garlic without coloring until soft, about 10 minutes. Add the beans and zucchini, season well and cook, stirring, for 1 minute.

3 Add the stock and bring to a boil, then simmer for 15 minutes or until the vegetables are just cooked, adding the peas after 5 minutes.

4 Add the rice and about two-thirds of the herbs and stir well. Simmer for 1–2 minutes until the rice is hot.

To Serve Taste for seasoning and ladle into warm soup plates. Sprinkle with the remaining herbs, garnish with the Parmesan shavings, and serve hot.

Chilled watercress soup

With its tangy bite, watercress makes a really good chilled soup, and you will see there is no need to enrich it with cream, as so many recipes do. Serve for a first course or a light lunch, with fresh granary or wholemeal rolls.

1 large Spanish onion

2 tablespoons butter

2⅔ cups diced floury potatoes

about 6¼ cups vegetable stock or water

pinch of freshly grated nutmeg

salt and freshly ground black pepper

6 cups roughly chopped watercress, plus 4 sprigs for garnish

Serves 4

Preparation time: 15–20 minutes, plus cooling and chilling time

Cooking time: 45 minutes

1   Finely chop the onion. Melt the butter in a large saucepan and sweat the onion over very low heat until soft but not colored, about 10 minutes.

2   Add the potatoes, stock or water, nutmeg, and salt and pepper to taste. Bring to a boil, cover, and simmer for about 30 minutes or until the potatoes are very soft.

3   Pour the soup into a food processor or blender, add the watercress and purée until smooth. Strain through a fine sieve into a bowl and leave to cool, then cover and chill in the refrigerator for at least 4 hours, preferably overnight.

To Serve   Stir the soup well and add a little more chilled stock if the consistency is too thick. Taste for seasoning. Ladle into chilled bowls and top each with a sprig of watercress. Serve well chilled.

Chef's Tips

Floury potatoes are used instead of cream to thicken the soup and make it velvety smooth. The best floury varieties are Desirée, King Edward and Maris Piper.

◆

Keep some stock in the refrigerator while chilling the soup in case you need some for thinning the soup down before serving.

◆

Variation

Serve the soup hot: after puréeing, return it to the rinsed pan and reheat until bubbling, stirring frequently. Add more stock if the consistency is too thick and stir until combined and heated through, then taste for seasoning.

CARROT AND CILANTRO SOUP

Cilantro plus coriander seeds give this popular smooth soup great depth of flavor. Serve it as a stylish starter in elegant wide-rimmed bowls – it looks especially good against white or blue.

1 lb carrots
1 onion
1 tablespoon coriander seeds
2 tablespoons butter
4 cups chicken or vegetable stock
a small handful of fresh cilantro
salt and freshly ground black pepper

Serves 4

Preparation time: 20 minutes
Cooking time: 40–45 minutes

1   Roughly chop the carrots. Thinly slice the onion. Crush the coriander seeds with a mortar and pestle.

2   Melt the butter in a large saucepan and sweat the onion over low heat for about 5 minutes until soft. Add the chopped carrots and crushed coriander seeds, stir well and sweat for another 5 minutes.

3   Add the stock, cilantro stalks, and salt and pepper to taste. Stir and bring to a boil, then cover and simmer for 25–30 minutes, or until the carrots are very soft.

4   Pour the soup into a food processor or blender and purée until smooth, then return to the rinsed pan and reheat. Meanwhile, chop the cilantro leaves.

To Serve   Taste the soup for seasoning, then ladle into warm bowls. Scatter the chopped cilantro over the surface of the soup and serve immediately.

Chef's Tip

To heighten the spiciness of the coriander seeds, dry-fry them before crushing them in step 1. Heat them in a non-stick frying pan over low to moderate heat for 2–3 minutes, stirring constantly with a wooden spoon. Once you can smell their toasted aroma, it is time to remove them from the heat. Tip them into the mortar and crush them while they are still hot.

CRAB AND TOMATO CHARLOTTES

These dainty little molded shapes are very quick and easy to make, and the orange and basil dressing is a really delicious flavor contrast. They are ideal for a dinner party because they can be prepared up to a day ahead.

1 lb large tomatoes

salt and freshly ground black pepper

¾ lb white crabmeat

½ cup half-fat crème fraîche

1 tablespoon tomato paste

2 teaspoons coarsegrain mustard

fresh basil leaves, to serve

Vinaigrette

4 sweet cherry tomatoes,
   preferably on the vine

1 handful of fresh basil leaves

4 tablespoons extra virgin olive oil

grated rind and juice of 1 orange

caster sugar, to taste (optional)

Serves 4

Preparation time: 15–20 minutes, plus chilling time

1   Line four ⅔ cup custard dishes with cling film, letting it hang over the edges.

2   Peel the large tomatoes, then slice them lengthwise into quarters and scrape out the cores and seeds. Cut a line across the center of each quarter, on the inside. This will make them more flexible. Line the ramekins with the tomato petal shapes, arranging them rounded side out and as close together as possible. Sprinkle with salt and pepper.

3   Mix the crab with the crème fraîche, tomato paste, mustard, and salt and pepper to taste. Spoon into the dishes and cover with the overhanging cling film. Chill in the refrigerator for at least 4 hours, preferably overnight.

4   When ready to serve, make the vinaigrette. Finely dice the cherry tomatoes and finely shred the basil. Place in a bowl with the oil, orange rind, and juice, and whisk together, then taste and season. Add a small amount of sugar if the tomatoes and orange are sharp.

To Serve   Unfold the cling film and place an inverted chilled plate on top of each dish. Turn the charlottes out onto the plates and remove the cling film. Spoon the dressing around the charlottes and scatter with basil leaves. Serve chilled.

Chef's Tips

You will need 5–6 large tomatoes to have enough quarters to line 4 ramekins. To peel them, cut a cross in the rounded ends and put the tomatoes in a bowl. Pour boiling water over the tomatoes, leave for 1–2 minutes until the skins start to peel back from the cuts, then drain and immerse in a bowl of cold water. The skins will peel off easily with your fingers.

◆

It is not always easy to get fresh white crabmeat. Two 6 oz cans of crabmeat can be used instead.

◆

Variation

Garnish the top of each charlotte with a tiny cluster of black lumpfish roe as well as the basil.

SMOKED TROUT WITH CUCUMBER AND CUMIN

Toasted cumin seeds give a spicy kick to the creamy dressing in this quick and easy Scandinavian-style starter. It can be prepared just before serving or several hours ahead. Served with nutty or seedy bread, it also makes an excellent lunch dish.

½ large cucumber
salt and freshly ground black pepper
1 tablespoon cumin seeds
8–10 oz smoked trout fillets
⅔ cup low-fat crème fraîche or plain yogurt

To Serve
about 6 cups baby salad leaves
fresh dill or chervil sprigs

Serves 4

Preparation time: 45 minutes, including standing time

Chef's Tip

Packets of baby salad leaves are available at supermarkets. Try to get a packet which contains some red leaves like chard, lollo rosso or radicchio. A few fresh herb leaves will add extra flavor – dill goes especially well with the other flavors in this dish.

◆

Variation

Use smoked salmon, mackerel, or eel instead of trout.

1   Peel the cucumber, cut it in half lengthwise and scoop out the seeds with a sharp-edged teaspoon. Cut the flesh into thin strips, place in a colander and sprinkle with salt. Leave for 30 minutes.

2   Meanwhile, dry-fry the cumin seeds in a non-stick frying pan for a few minutes until toasted. Flake the trout into large pieces.

3   Rinse the cucumber under the cold tap, drain, and pat dry with paper towels. Place in a bowl, sprinkle the toasted cumin seeds over the top, and mix in the crème fraîche or yogurt. Season with pepper to taste.

To Serve   Tear the salad leaves into bite-size pieces and arrange like nests around the edges of 4 plates. Spoon the cucumber mixture into the center. Pile the trout attractively on top of the cucumber and garnish with sprigs of dill or chervil. Serve at room temperature.

HOT CRAB AND GINGER SOUFFLÉS

Crab and ginger are a favorite combination of flavors in the Far East. Here they're used with great success in a classic French soufflé recipe. Individual soufflés are easier to make than large ones because they are less likely to sink in the middle.

2 tablespoons butter

¼ cup dried white breadcrumbs

3 tablespoons pickled ginger

¼ cup all-purpose flour

1¼ cups hot milk

7 oz crabmeat (brown and white)

4 eggs, separated

salt and freshly ground black pepper

Serves 4

Preparation time: 20 minutes
Cooking time: 15–20 minutes

Chef's Tips

Pungent pickled ginger, also called sushi ginger, is sold in jars at Japanese stores and in the oriental sections of large supermarkets. It is fresh root ginger that has been peeled, very thinly sliced and pickled in rice vinegar.

◆

If you can't get fresh brown and white crabmeat, use cans of dressed crab, which are white and brown meat mixed together.

1   Preheat the oven to 375°F. Butter the insides of four 1-cup soufflé dishes and coat with dried breadcrumbs. Finely chop the pickled ginger.

2   Melt the remaining butter in a saucepan, add the flour, and stir over low to moderate heat for 1 minute. Stir in the pickled ginger and gradually whisk in the milk. Bring to a boil, stirring, then simmer for 2 minutes.

3   Remove the pan from the heat and stir in the crabmeat and egg yolks. Season well.

4   In a clean bowl, whisk the egg whites until stiff. Fold into the crab mixture, then spoon into the prepared dishes and run the tip of a blunt knife around the inside of the rims. This will facilitate rising. Bake for 15–20 minutes or until risen and golden.

To Serve   Quickly transfer the dishes to small plates and serve immediately.

Spiced shrimp and squid skewers

This Asian-inspired dish is given extra flavor by being cooked on the barbecue, but it can equally well be cooked under the broiler, or on a ridged, cast-iron grill pan on top of the stove.

16 large raw shrimp in their shells

7 oz prepared baby squid

2 tablespoons sesame seeds

Marinade

1 inch piece of fresh root ginger

2 garlic cloves

1 tablespoon light soy sauce

1 tablespoon sweet sherry

1 teaspoon chili oil

1 tablespoon cornstarch

To Serve

about 6 cups mixed salad leaves

juice of 1 lime

lime wedges

Serves 4

Preparation time: 20 minutes, plus marinating time

Cooking time: 6–8 minutes

Chef's Tips

You can buy ready prepared whole baby squid pouches from supermarkets. Don't buy squid rings because they are difficult to thread on skewers.

◆

Wrap fresh root ginger well and keep it in the freezer. When it is frozen hard, ginger is very easy to peel and grate.

◆

Chili oil is available from Chinese and Indian shops and the oriental sections of supermarkets. Made with dried red chilies, it is bright orange and fiery hot. If you prefer an oil with a milder taste, use sesame oil.

1   First make the marinade. Peel and grate the ginger into a large bowl. Crush the garlic and add to the ginger with the remaining marinade ingredients. Whisk well to mix.

2   Remove the shells from the shrimp and cut the squid into 1 inch pieces. Add the shrimp and squid to the marinade and stir to mix, then cover and marinate in the refrigerator for up to 4 hours.

3   Soak 8 short wooden skewers in a bowl of warm water for at least 30 minutes. Prepare the barbecue for cooking.

4   Add the sesame seeds to the fish and marinade and stir to coat evenly, then thread the shrimp and squid alternately on the drained skewers. Spoon over any marinade and barbecue for 3–4 minutes on each side.

To Serve   Arrange a small bed of salad leaves on each plate and top with the skewers of fish. Squeeze a little lime juice over the skewers and serve immediately, with lime wedges as a garnish.

CHINESE PICKLED VEGETABLES WITH CHILI DIP

This is an excellent starter for an oriental meal and it needs to be made well ahead of time, so it is good for entertaining. Tell your guests to put a little of the chili dip on the side of their plates and to taste it with caution to begin with.

1 cup diced carrot

1 cup diced mooli

1 cup canned water chestnuts, chopped

4 tablespoons rice vinegar

4 cups shredded Chinese leaves, to serve

Dip

3 mild red chilies

2 oz pickled ginger

1 teaspoon tomato paste

Serves 4

Preparation time: 15 minutes, plus marinating time

Chef's Tips

Mooli is Japanese white radish, sometimes called daikon. You can get it in most supermarkets, and Asian stores of course. Its beauty lies in its pure white flesh, which has a very crisp texture when raw.

◆

Water chestnuts are not chestnuts at all, but crisp white bulbs with a brown skin. Canned water chestnuts are peeled and ready to eat, either raw or heated through in stir-fries.

◆

When buying red chilies, the larger and fatter they are the milder they are most likely to be. The very tiny, skinny ones are usually the hottest.

1   Mix all the vegetables together with the rice vinegar. Cover and set aside for 2–3 hours, mixing occasionally.

2   Meanwhile, halve and deseed the chilies, then pound them to a paste with the pickled ginger. Use a pestle and mortar for pounding, or the small bowl and blade of a food processor. Mix in the tomato paste and turn into a small serving bowl.

To Serve   Pile up the Chinese leaves on a plate. Drain the pickled vegetables and place on top of the leaves. Serve at room temperature, with the bowl of chili dip alongside.

EGGPLANT AND CUMIN DIP

This is similar to the Middle Eastern eggplant dip, baba ghanoush. It has a creamy consistency and a smoky flavor laced with garlic, and is delicious in summer served with fresh vegetable crudités or pita bread.

3 large eggplants, total weight about 1½ lb

4 teaspoons olive oil

2 shallots

2 garlic cloves

½ teaspoon cumin seeds

1 scant cup Greek yogurt

salt and freshly ground black pepper

To Serve

about 1 tablespoon extra virgin olive oil

pinch of paprika

Serves 4–6

Preparation time: 20 minutes, plus chilling time

Cooking time: 45 minutes

Chef's Tip

Greek yogurt comes in 3 different varieties. When it is made with cow's milk, it is available with 10% fat or fat-free. Made with sheep's milk, it usually contains about 6% fat. You can use any of these in this recipe, according to personal taste. The cow's milk yogurt containing 10% fat will give the creamiest result; the other two yogurts will give the dip a slightly sharper taste.

◆

Variation

Halve, deseed and finely chop 1 mild green chili, then fry with the shallots in step 3.

1   Preheat the oven to 350°F. Cut the eggplants in half lengthwise and score a criss-cross pattern in the flesh. Place the eggplants cut side up on a cookie sheet and brush with half the oil. Bake for 45 minutes, or until the flesh is soft, especially around the edges.

2   Remove the eggplants from the oven and leave for a while until they are cool enough to handle.

3   Meanwhile, finely chop the shallots and crush the garlic. Heat the remaining oil in a non-stick skillet, add the shallots and garlic, and stir over low heat for a few minutes until softened. Turn into a food processor. Add the cumin seeds to the skillet and fry for a few minutes until toasted, then tip them into the food processor.

4   Scoop the eggplant flesh out of the skins into the food processor. Add the yogurt and work to a purée, then add salt and pepper to taste. Turn the dip into a shallow serving dish and swirl the surface to make it level. Cover and chill in the refrigerator for at least 4 hours.

To Serve   Drizzle a little oil over the surface of the the dip and sprinkle with paprika. Serve chilled.

ROAST RED BELL PEPPER PÂTÉ

Intensely flavored with smoky roast vegetables and garlic, this pâté-cum-dip is at its best served with a selection of brightly colored, crisp crudités and warm pita bread. Make it for a summer barbecue party when bell peppers and tomatoes are plentiful and cheap.

1 lb red bell peppers

1 lb ripe plum tomatoes

1–2 tablespoons olive oil

3 garlic cloves in their skins

1 handful of fresh basil leaves

1 teaspoon sea salt

2–3 teaspoons lemon juice

freshly ground black pepper

a few fresh basil leaves, to serve

Serves 4

Preparation time: 30 minutes, plus cooling, chilling and bringing to room temperature
Cooking time: 1½ hours

Chef's Tips

Plum tomatoes are the ones used for canning, but they are widely available fresh as well. When ripe, they are good for roasting because they have a good color, rich flavor, and juicy flesh. The best kind are the ones that have been ripened on the vine in the sun, and these are easy to get in the summer and early fall.

◆

A little goes a long way with this pâté because it has a strong flavor. The quantities given here are ample for 4 people, but you can easily double or triple the recipe if you want to make more.

1   Preheat the oven to 325°F. Cut the bell peppers and tomatoes in half lengthwise and remove the cores and seeds. Place the peppers and tomatoes in a large roasting pan and sprinkle with 1 tablespoon oil. Roast for 1½ hours, stirring and turning occasionally, and add the garlic cloves for the last 30 minutes.

2   Allow the vegetables to cool, then peel off and discard the skins from the peppers and garlic. Put the vegetables in a food processor and add the basil and salt. Work to a rough paste, then add another tablespoon of oil, and lemon juice and pepper to taste. If the mixture is not moist enough, add some of the roasting juices from the vegetables.

3   Transfer the mixture to a serving bowl, cover tightly with cling film and chill in the refrigerator for at least 4 hours, preferably overnight.

To Serve   Let stand at room temperature for about 30 minutes, then unwrap and scatter with basil leaves.

CHICKEN AND VEGETABLE SPRING ROLLS

Spring rolls are usually deep fried, but these are the uncooked type made from rice paper, so they are lighter and healthier. The contrast between the soft wrappers and the shredded filling is extremely good.

1 carrot	*Dipping Sauce*	Serves 4
3 celery sticks	1 red chili	
4 scallions	1 scallion	Preparation time: 30–40 minutes
1 small smoked chicken breast	1 teaspoon grated fresh root ginger	
2 garlic cloves	4 tablespoons light soy sauce	
1 inch piece of fresh root ginger	1 tablespoon sesame oil	
2 tablespoons chopped fresh	1 tablespoon clear honey	
cilantro	1 tablespoon rice or	
10 round rice paper wrappers	white wine vinegar	
	juice of 1 lime	

1   Very finely shred the carrot, celery, and scallions into julienne strips. Blanch the carrot and celery in boiling water for 1–2 minutes, until just softened. Drain and plunge into cold water, then drain well.

2   Shred the chicken, discarding the skin and any bones, and place in a bowl. Finely chop the garlic and add to the chicken, then peel and grate the ginger into the bowl. Add the blanched vegetables, scallions, and cilantro. Mix well.

3   Dip a sheet of rice paper in a bowl of warm water for 10–20 seconds, then place about 3 tablespoons of the filling in the center. Fold in the sides of the paper, then roll it up in the opposite direction to make a cylindrical parcel. Seal the open edge with water and place the parcel seam-side down on a damp cloth. Cover with another damp cloth and repeat until all the ingredients are used.

4   Make the dipping sauce. Very finely shred the chili (removing the seeds if you prefer) and the scallion. Set aside a few pieces for garnish, then mix the rest with the remaining sauce ingredients.

To Serve   Arrange the spring rolls with the bowl of dipping sauce and garnish with the reserved shredded chili and scallion.

Chef's Tip

Rice paper wrappers are translucent white and round, usually about 8½ inches in diameter. You can buy them, fresh or frozen, at oriental stores. They do not need cooking, but they are brittle when you buy them so they must be dipped in water to make them soft enough to roll. To prevent them drying out during preparation, always keep them well covered with a damp cloth, as you would with phyllo pastry.

◆

Variation

If you find smoked chicken difficult to get, you can use smoked duck instead – or ordinary roast or poached chicken.

BLACKENED CORN WITH CHIVE VINAIGRETTE

A recipe for the fall when corn is at its sweetest and best. Serve as a first course with crusty French bread to mop up the tangy dressing. Pierce the ends of the corn with small skewers and provide plenty of paper napkins.

4 corn cobs
sea or rock salt and freshly ground black pepper

Chive Vinaigrette
½ cup extra virgin olive oil
grated rind and juice of 1 lemon
2 tablespoons chopped fresh chives

Serves 4

Preparation time: 10 minutes
Cooking time: 15 minutes

1   Preheat the broiler to hot. Remove the papery husks, silks, and fibers from the outside of the corn cobs and place the corn under the broiler for about 15 minutes, turning several times until the corn is mottled black and charred.

2   Meanwhile, whisk together the ingredients for the vinaigrette.

To Serve   Remove the corn from the broiler and place on plates. Spoon the chive vinaigrette over the hot corn and sprinkle generously with salt and pepper. Serve hot.

Chef's Tips

Never add salt to the water for boiling corn because it toughens the kernels. For a sweeter flavor, add a pinch or two of sugar if you like.

◆

Use best quality extra virgin olive oil for dressings like this one in which the flavor is of paramount importance. Keep a bottle especially for salads and for sprinkling over cooked foods just before serving. Check the label: it should say "cold-pressed" or "from the first cold pressing." This type of olive oil tastes fruity; some kinds are peppery hot.

SPICY CHEESE, TOMATO, AND BASIL SOUFFLÉS

Sun-dried tomatoes and basil give these summery little soufflés a
Mediterranean flavor, while chili and Parmesan give them a spicy kick.
They are good served with warm olive or tomato ciabatta.

a little softened butter, for coating

½ cup finely grated Parmesan cheese

1 teaspoon mild chili powder

4 pieces of sun-dried tomato

4 eggs, separated

2 tablespoons dry white wine

1 tablespoon tomato juice

salt and freshly ground black pepper

1 tablespoon shredded fresh basil

4 small fresh basil sprigs, to serve

Serves 4

Preparation time: 20–30 minutes
Cooking time: 8–10 minutes

Chef's Tip

This recipe uses the kind of sun-dried tomatoes you buy in packages. They are soaked in water before use to make them easier to chop and less chewy. If you prefer, you can use sun-dried tomatoes which are packed in olive oil. These do not need soaking before use, but they should be drained on paper towels to remove excess oil.

1   Preheat the oven to 425°F. Butter the insides of four 1-cup soufflé
dishes. Mix the Parmesan and chili powder together, put 1 tablespoon
of this mixture into each dish and turn to coat the inside thoroughly.

2   Put the sun-dried tomato pieces in a bowl, cover with boiling
water and set aside. Put the egg yolks and wine in a heatproof bowl
over a pan of hot water. Whisk until thick and foamy, remove from the
heat and stir in the tomato juice and seasoning to taste.

3   Drain the sun-dried tomatoes well, squeeze out as much excess
water as possible, then finely chop them.

4   In a clean bowl, whisk the egg whites until stiff. Fold them into
the yolk mixture with the sun-dried tomatoes, basil, and the remaining
spiced Parmesan. Spoon into the prepared dishes and run the tip of a
blunt knife around the inside of the rims. This will facilitate rising.
Bake in the oven for 8–10 minutes or until risen and golden.

To Serve   Quickly transfer the dishes to small plates, garnish with basil
sprigs and serve immediately.

2

FISH
& SHELLFISH

It is hard to beat fish and shellfish for low-fat protein. They are both lighter and easier to digest than poultry and meat – and quicker to cook. Oily fish has the added bonus of containing unsaturated oils, and these can help prevent heart disease if eaten regularly. Fish and shellfish deserve to be eaten more often.

The recipes in this chapter concentrate on the healthier methods of cooking fish – poaching, baking, broiling, barbecuing, and chargrilling in a cast-iron pan. Fat is kept to a minimum with these cooking methods and yet the end results are beautifully tender, tasty, and moist. The secret is not to overcook, because the delicate flesh of fish and shellfish quickly becomes dry. Always cook for the least amount of time and err on the side of caution. Remember that the flesh continues to cook in its own heat for a while after the fish is removed from the oven or hob.

The variety and choice of fish and shellfish are forever increasing and many are interchangeable in recipes. Fishmongers are immensely knowledgeable, and usually more than happy to give advice about what is best to buy on the day. If you don't see what you want, ask your fishmonger to recommend an alternative. This is far better than sticking rigidly to a recipe. Your fishmonger will know this, and will also prepare fish ready for cooking at no extra charge.

OPEN RAVIOLI OF RED MULLET

Squares of fresh lasagne are stacked on top of each other with diamonds of red mullet in between and fresh green vegetables all around. The dish is served like a warm salad, with a drizzle of cool basil vinaigrette.

1½ lb young lima beans in their pods

1 small zucchini

12 red mullet fillets, skinned

2 teaspoons olive oil

6 sheets of fresh lasagne

fresh basil leaves, to serve

Basil Vinaigrette

2 cups fresh basil leaves

4 tablespoons extra virgin olive oil

1 tablespoon lemon juice

salt and freshly ground black pepper

½ teaspoon sugar

Serves 4

Preparation time: 30 minutes

Cooking time: about 15 minutes

Chef's Tip

For a very special chef's garnish, thinly slice 1 small black truffle and arrange the slices decoratively on top of the pasta just before serving.

1   Preheat the oven to 300°F. Make the vinaigrette. Purée the basil and oil in a food processor or blender, adding the lemon juice towards the end. Season with salt and pepper and set aside.

2   Shell the beans and thinly slice the zucchini. Cut each mullet fillet diagonally into 2–3 diamond shapes and season. Heat the oil in a non-stick skillet and pan-fry the fish, skin-side up, for 2–3 minutes. Transfer the fish, skin-side up, to an oiled cookie sheet, cover with foil and place in the oven for 5 minutes to finish cooking.

3   Blanch the beans and zucchini in boiling water for 2 minutes. Drain both vegetables and skin the beans. Place the vegetables in a heatproof dish, cover, and keep warm in the oven.

4   Cut the pasta sheets in half to make shapes that are roughly square. Cook in a large saucepan of salted boiling water for 3–4 minutes or until al dente. Drain well and place in a single layer on a clean cloth.

To Serve   Layer the pasta and fish on 4 warm plates, starting and finishing with pasta and letting the fish peep out. Scatter the beans and zucchini around. Mix the sugar into the vinaigrette, spoon it over and around, then grind black pepper over the top. Garnish with basil leaves and serve immediately.

WARM SALAD OF SMOKED SALMON AND SORREL

This is a dish of contrasting colors, textures, and flavors which complement each other superbly well. The saltiness of smoked salmon, sweetness of pink grapefruit, and sharpness of sorrel taste very good together. Serve for a light lunch, with crusty bread.

2 pink grapefruit

14 oz–1 lb smoked salmon

6 black peppercorns

1 bay leaf

6 cups shredded sorrel leaves

4 tablespoons extra virgin olive oil

salt and freshly ground black pepper

Serves 4

Preparation time: 15–20 minutes
Cooking time: 5–7 minutes

1   Preheat the oven to 350°F. Cut 3 long strips of peel from one of the grapefruit, avoiding the white pith. Put the strips in a shallow baking dish. Peel both fruit totally, cutting off and discarding all the remaining peel and pith. Segment the grapefruit over a bowl, catching the juice. Place the segments in another large bowl.

2   Place the smoked salmon, peppercorns, and bay leaf in the baking dish. Pour cold water over the fish to just cover it, then bake in the oven for 5–7 minutes, or until the fish has just turned pale.

3   Remove the salmon with a slotted spoon and discard the cooking liquid, grapefruit peel, and flavorings. Drain the salmon well and add it to the bowl of grapefruit segments with the sorrel. Fold the ingredients very gently together until evenly combined.

4   Whisk the oil in a jug with 3 tablespoons of the reserved grapefruit juice and season generously with pepper. Drizzle the dressing over the salad and toss gently.

To Serve   Turn the salad into a serving bowl and serve immediately.

Chef's Tip

Don't buy expensive, perfect slices of smoked salmon. Smoked salmon trimmings, sometimes called cocktail salmon, are good enough for cooking, and they are much cheaper than the slices.

◆

Variations

If you prefer a milder flavor for the dressing, use half olive oil and half sunflower oil.

◆

If sorrel is difficult to find, use watercress instead. It will give the salad a more peppery bite than sorrel. Cut off and discard the ends of the watercress stalks, then tear the rest of the watercress into small sprigs.

◆

If you have a bottle of dry white wine open, use it to cook the smoked salmon rather than water, or use half wine and half water.

MACKEREL WITH PEANUTS AND CHILIES

The robust flavors of scallions, garlic, and chilies hold their own against mackerel, a fish with a strong flavor. The mackerel looks and tastes good served Asian-style, broken into large pieces on a mound of fragrant jasmine rice.

8 mackerel fillets

4 scallions

½ cup natural unsalted peanuts, skinned

2 green chilies

1 garlic clove

2 tablespoons peanut oil

salt

lime or lemon wedges, to serve

Serves 4

Preparation time: 10–15 minutes, plus marinating time
Cooking time: 6–8 minutes

Variation

For a different serving idea, arrange the mackerel fillets on a bed of noodles. Soak 7 oz Chinese dried cellophane noodles in 4 cups boiling vegetable stock or water for 3 minutes and drain thoroughly before serving.

1   Cut several slits in a lattice pattern in the mackerel skin. Place skin-side down on a non-metallic tray. Remove the green tops from the scallions and cut into fine strips. Place these in iced water in the refrigerator and reserve for the garnish. Thinly slice the white parts of the scallions and scatter over the fish.

2   Crush the peanuts with the flat side of a large knife blade. Halve, deseed, and finely chop the chilies. Crush the garlic.

3   Sprinkle the peanuts, chilies, and garlic over the fish, drizzle half of the oil over, and sprinkle with a little salt. Cover and set aside at cool room temperature for 1 hour, turning once.

4   Preheat the broiler or prepare the barbecue for cooking. Brush the fish with the remaining oil and broil or barbecue for 3–4 minutes on each side, or until cooked through.

To Serve   Transfer the fish to warm plates and garnish with the drained scallion tassels. Serve hot, with lime or lemon wedges for squeezing.

SALMON IN VODKA WITH RED CABBAGE

This is an inspired dish from northern Europe. It combines traditional sweet and sour red cabbage braised with onion, apple, sugar, and wine with the delicate flavor of salmon. Serve it for a dinner party main course, with new potatoes or Mash (page 187).

4 thick salmon fillets, each weighing
  5–6 oz, skinned
½ cup vodka
4 tablespoons cold fish stock
2 tablespoons chopped fresh dill
6 cups finely shredded red cabbage
salt and freshly ground black pepper
1 red onion

2 garlic cloves
1 small cooking apple
2 tablespoons butter
1 tablespoon soft brown sugar
⅓ cup red wine
4 fresh dill sprigs, to serve

Serves 4

Preparation time: 30–60 minutes, including marinating time
Cooking time: 30–35 minutes

Chef's Tip

Look for wild salmon at the fishmonger or supermarket. It has more flavor than farmed salmon, which tends to be bland, but it is more expensive. For a special occasion, you will find it well worth the extra cost.

1   Make sure all the bones in the fish have been removed, then place the fish in a shallow, non-metallic baking dish. Mix the vodka, stock, and dill together, pour over the fish and cover with cling film. Marinate in the refrigerator for 30–60 minutes.

2   Place the red cabbage in a colander and sprinkle with salt. Finely chop the onion and crush the garlic. Peel, core, and finely chop the apple.

3   Preheat the oven to 350°F. Melt the butter in a large saucepan and sweat the onion and garlic over low heat until soft. Rinse the cabbage and shake off the excess water, then add the cabbage to the pan with the apple, sugar, pepper to taste, wine, and ⅓ cup cold water. Cook for 3 minutes, stirring, then cover and cook, stirring occasionally, for about 25 minutes until the liquid has been absorbed. The cabbage should be tender but still a little crisp.

4   Meanwhile, uncover the dish of salmon, place it in the oven and bake for 15 minutes, or until just cooked.

To Serve Place the red cabbage on warm plates, arrange the salmon on top, and spoon over the cooking liquid. Garnish each serving with a sprig of dill and serve immediately.

PLAICE WITH WILD MUSHROOMS

Simple and quick, this dish is given a wild earthy flavor from the mushrooms, which also make it more satisfying. Here, chanterelles, girolles, and trompettes des morts are used for color and flavor contrast, but you can use any type of mushroom you like.

2 shallots

1¼ cups fish stock

½ cup dry white wine

1 bouquet garni

a little butter

salt and freshly ground black pepper

12 small plaice fillets, skinned

1 cup sliced wild or exotic
  mushrooms

1 tablespoon low-fat crème fraîche

lemon juice

2–3 tablespoons chopped
  fresh parsley

fresh flat-leaf parsley sprigs, to serve

Serves 4

Preparation time: 10–15 minutes

Cooking time: 20 minutes

1   Preheat the oven to 375°F. Finely chop the shallots. Put the stock, wine, and bouquet garni into a saucepan. Add 1¼ cups cold water, bring to a boil, and boil until reduced to 1¾ cups.

2   Meanwhile, butter a shallow flameproof dish. Season the fish, fold each fillet into three, skinned side inwards, and place in the dish. Sprinkle the shallots and mushrooms over the fish.

3   Strain the stock into the dish. Bring to a boil, cover, and place in the oven. Bake for 5–8 minutes or until the fish is white. Transfer the fish to a warm platter, leaving the mushrooms and shallots behind. Cover the fish and keep hot.

4   Boil the sauce for a few minutes, stirring constantly until reduced. Add the crème fraîche, a squeeze of lemon juice, and 2 tablespoons parsley. Stir to mix, then taste for seasoning and add more lemon juice and parsley if you like.

To Serve   Coat the fish with the sauce, garnish with parsley sprigs, and serve immediately.

Chef's Tips

There is a recipe for a light fish stock on page 180, but if you don't have the time to make your own, use chilled fresh or canned fish stock, available at most supermarkets and delicatessens. Both of these have a very good flavor, and are better than using stock cubes.

◆

You will need 3 whole plaice to get 12 fillets. If they are very small you may prefer to leave the skin on because it is very fiddly to remove and may tear the delicate flesh of the plaice.

◆

Variation

For a special occasion, use lemon sole instead of plaice.

COD AND BABY VEGETABLES EN PAPILLOTE

There is hardly any fat at all in this dish, making it ideal when you are entertaining guests who are on low-fat diets. It is easy to manage too, because it can be prepared in advance and popped in the oven while you are eating the first course.

7 oz mixed baby vegetables	*Dressing*
3½ oz sugarsnap peas	grated rind and juice of ½ small orange
3½ oz baby new potatoes	juice of 1 small lemon
4 cod steaks, each weighing about	1 tablespoon chopped fresh cilantro
7 oz	1 teaspoon crushed Sichuan
salt and freshly ground black pepper	peppercorns
1 tablespoon chilled butter	¼ teaspoon sea salt

Serves 4

Preparation time: 20 minutes
Cooking time: 40 minutes

1   Preheat the oven to 375°F. Put a large saucepan of water on to boil. Trim the vegetables if necessary and halve them if they are not tiny. Cut 4 large circles of baking parchment and foil, about 12 inches in diameter. Place a circle of paper over a circle of foil, then place a piece of fish on top, just off center. Season. Repeat with the remaining circles and fish.

2   Add salt to the water, then boil each type of vegetable separately for 2–3 minutes until just tender. The potatoes may take a little longer. Remove to a colander with a slotted spoon.

3   Mix all the dressing ingredients and taste for seasoning. Put the vegetables on top of the fish and spoon the dressing over them (you may not need all of it). Dice the butter and scatter over the vegetables, then fold the paper and foil over to make half-moon shapes. Fold and pleat the edges so they are sealed and there are 4 neat parcels.

4   Put the parcels on a cookie sheet and bake for 20–25 minutes, depending on the thickness of the fish. Open up the parcels for 5 minutes at the end.

To Serve   Place a parcel on each of 4 plates, or remove the fish and vegetables from the parcels and place them on warm plates, whichever you prefer.

Chef's Tips

For color and flavor contrast, the best baby vegetables for this dish are turnips, carrots, and zucchini. When buying the new potatoes, choose the smallest you can find.

◆

If you prefer, you can double wrap the fish and vegetables in the baking parchment. This looks more attractive than foil.

◆

Variation

You can use other fish besides cod. Haddock, hake, and salmon are all suitable, or a more unusual fish like red mullet or sea bream.

MONKFISH IN NORI

Nori seaweed protects the delicate flesh of fish during roasting in the oven. It is used here as a tasty low-fat alternative to bacon rashers, which are often wrapped around monkfish for roasting.

2 monkfish tails, each weighing about 1½ lb, filleted (see Chef's Tips)

2 red-hot chilies

finely grated rind and juice of 1 lime

½ cup mirin

2 tablespoons rice vinegar

1 tablespoon light soy sauce

2 tablespoons sesame oil

1 x 1oz package dried nori

Serves 4

Preparation time: 20 minutes, plus marinating time
Cooking time: 15–20 minutes

Chef's Tips

Monkfish tails come with a central bone running through them. Ask your fishmonger to remove the bone from each tail – he will cut the tails lengthwise in two so you will have 4 pieces of fish altogether. The tough membrane can be removed at the same time.

◆

Mirin is sweet rice wine. You can buy it in Japanese shops and the oriental sections of supermarkets.

◆

Nori is a Japanese seaweed rich in vitamins and minerals. It is sold as dried roasted sheets in packages in the oriental sections of supermarkets and at health food stores. Sheets of nori are shiny and dark green, like stiff crinkled paper. For this recipe they need to be dampened so they are pliable enough to wrap around the fish.

1   Remove any skin and membrane from the 4 pieces of monkfish, if this has not already been done. Place the fish in a shallow, non-metallic dish. Halve, deseed, and finely chop the chilies, then mix them with the lime rind and juice, mirin, vinegar, soy sauce, and half the sesame oil. Pour over the fish, cover with cling film, and marinate in the refrigerator for about 1 hour.

2   Preheat the oven to 350°F. Dampen 3 sheets of nori and lay them flat on a board. Overlap them slightly so there are no gaps in between. Lift one of the monkfish fillets out of the marinade and place it on the nori, then wrap the nori around the fish, leaving a little room for the fish to swell. Place the parcel in a baking dish. Repeat with the remaining nori and fish, reserving the marinade.

3   Brush the parcels with the remaining oil and bake in the oven for 15–20 minutes. To test for doneness, pierce the fish through the nori with a skewer. The fish should feel tender but still slightly firm. Remove the fish from the oven and pour the cooking juices into a saucepan. Add the reserved marinade, bring to a boil, and simmer for a few minutes.

To Serve   Slice the parcels of fish crosswise with a very sharp knife. Arrange the slices on warm plates, spoon the sauce over, and serve.

TUNA WITH BOK CHOI AND MUSHROOMS

Tuna is meaty and satisfying, yet very low in fat. It needs only an hour to marinate in this recipe, then all you have to do is quickly chargrill it and stir-fry the vegetables, making this an ideal dish for entertaining at short notice.

4 pieces of tuna fillet, each weighing 5–6 oz

3 red-hot fresh chilies

2 garlic cloves

1 cup red wine

10 oz bok choi

1 cup button mushrooms

salt and freshly ground black pepper

1 tablespoon olive oil

Serves 4

Preparation time: 15 minutes, plus marinating time
Cooking time: 6–8 minutes

1   Place the pieces of tuna in a single layer in a non-metallic dish. Thinly slice the chilies and garlic, sprinkle them over the tuna, and pour in the wine. Cover and marinate in the refrigerator for 1 hour. Meanwhile, coarsely chop the bok choi (both the stalks and the leaves) and halve the mushrooms lengthwise.

2   When ready to cook, heat a ridged, cast-iron grill pan until very hot. Lift the tuna out of the marinade, drain on paper towel, and season with a little salt. Pour the marinade into a small pan, add salt and pepper to taste, then simmer for a few minutes until reduced by about half. Remove from the heat, cover, and keep hot.

3   Dip a wad of paper towels in oil and wipe it over the hot grill pan. Place the tuna on the pan and chargrill it until done to your liking, about 3 minutes on each side for rare in the center, 4 minutes on each side for medium to well-done.

4   Meanwhile, heat the remaining oil in a wok or large deep frying pan until very hot. Add the bok choi and mushrooms and stir-fry over high heat for about 3 minutes. Season.

To Serve   Cut the pieces of tuna in half. Mound the vegetables on warm plates, and top with the tuna and marinade. Serve hot.

Chef's Tip

Bok choi, sometimes spelled bok choy or called pak choi, is a member of the cabbage family. You can get it in oriental supermarkets, although many supermarkets also stock it. It is easy to recognize by its thick, creamy white stalks and dark green leaves. It has a mild, peppery taste.

◆

Variation

If you prefer not to chargrill the fish and stir-fry the vegetables at the last moment, this dish can be made in another way that does not involve last-minute cooking. Chargrill the tuna for 3 minutes on each side until pink in the center, place in the marinade and leave to cool, then chill for several hours in the refrigerator. Serve cold on a bed of raw mushrooms and bok choi, with the marinade poured over.

Herbed phyllo sole parcels with tomato sauce

This is a delicate-looking main course. Serve with new potatoes tossed in chopped fresh herbs, extra virgin olive oil, and a drop or two of balsamic vinegar. A fresh vegetable like snow peas or sugarsnap peas would also be nice.

2 cups button mushrooms

4 tablespoons olive oil

juice of ½ lemon

salt and freshly ground black pepper

8 rectangular sheets of phyllo pastry

2 heaped tablespoons fresh
    chervil leaves

4 sole fillets

Tomato Sauce

1¼ cups tomato juice

1 teaspoon finely chopped fresh
    tarragon

¼ cup fresh white breadcrumbs

Serves 4

Preparation time: 30 minutes

Cooking time: 15 minutes

Chef's Tips

The most convenient way to buy phyllo pastry is frozen. It is available in boxes at supermarkets and Middle Eastern stores. The exact size of the phyllo sheets is not important for this recipe. Once the sheets have thawed, cover them with cling film or a damp cloth to prevent them drying out.

◆

Use lemon sole. It is less expensive than Dover sole, and easier to find.

◆

Buy a carton or bottle of natural tomato juice, the type you would normally buy for drinking. It is concentrated and strained so the consistency is rich and smooth, ideal for making sauces. Check the label to see if salt has been added and take care with the seasoning.

1   Preheat the oven to 400°F. Finely chop the mushrooms. Heat 1 tablespoon of the oil in a sauté pan, add the mushrooms and lemon juice and cook over low to moderate heat for 3–4 minutes until completely dry. Season.

2   Lay 1 sheet of phyllo flat on the work surface and brush with oil. Lay one-quarter of the chervil leaves on top, spreading them out in an even pattern. Cover with another sheet of phyllo and brush with oil.

3   Pat a fish fillet dry and place it lengthwise on the pastry. Season the fish and top with one-quarter of the mushroom mixture, then fold in the 2 short sides of the pastry. Fold in the 2 long sides, then place the parcel, seam-side down, on a cookie sheet and brush with more oil. Repeat with the remaining pastry, chervil, and fish.

4   Bake for 15 minutes or until the pastry is golden around the edges and the fish is tender in the center when pierced through the pastry with a skewer. Meanwhile, gently heat the tomato juice, tarragon, and breadcrumbs in a small pan, whisking until smooth and thickened. Remove from the heat and add salt and pepper to taste.

To Serve   Place the fish parcels on warm plates and spoon the sauce alongside. Serve hot.

SALMON FISH CAKES WITH LEMON AND DILL

Homemade fish cakes are far superior to any that you can buy. For one thing, you can be sure of what's in them. These are extra tasty because they are packed with fresh salmon and herbs and served with a tangy, yogurt-based sauce.

10 oz salmon fillet
½ cup hot fish stock
½–⅔ cup hot low-fat milk
3 baked potatoes
2 tablespoons chopped fresh dill
2 tablespoons chopped fresh parsley
salt and freshly ground black pepper
1 egg yolk
2 eggs

about 1 cup dried breadcrumbs
lemon wedges, to serve

Dressing
1 scant cup low-fat plain yogurt
finely grated rind of 1 lemon
¼ bunch of fresh dill

Makes 8

Preparation time: 40 minutes
Cooking time: 1½–1¾ hours,
including baking time for potatoes

Chef's Tips

The best potatoes for baking are the large, floury main-crop types. These have a light and fluffy texture when cooked. To bake potatoes, prick them in several places with a skewer or fork, then bake in a 400° oven for 1¼ hours or until tender.

The fish cakes can be prepared up to the end of step 3, then kept in the refrigerator for up to 24 hours before cooking. If you refrigerate them uncovered, the breadcrumb coating will harden and be extra crisp when baked.

1   Preheat the oven to 375°F. Put the salmon in a baking dish with the stock and ½ cup of the milk. Cover with foil and poach in the oven for 5–6 minutes, or until the fish flakes easily with a fork. Remove the fish with a slotted spoon and drain on paper towels.

2   Flake the fish, discarding the skin and any bones. Cut the baked potatoes in half, then scoop out the flesh and mash with a fork. Add the fish and herbs to the potato and mix thoroughly. Season well with salt and pepper and moisten with the egg yolk. Add a little milk if the mixture seems dry.

3   Divide the mixture into 8 equal pieces and pat into small cakes. Beat the eggs in a shallow dish with a pinch each of salt and pepper. Coat the fish cakes with beaten egg mixture, then the breadcrumbs.

4   Place the fish cakes on a baking pan and bake for 15 minutes or until golden, turning them over halfway. Meanwhile, mix the yogurt, lemon rind, and dill together to make the dressing.

To Serve   Place the fish cakes on a warm platter with the bowl of dressing in the center. Garnish with lemon wedges and serve.

SALMON AND SCALLOP WRAPS

This is a very special dish for a dinner party. If you are lucky enough to buy scallops with the orange coral (roe) attached, these can be pulled off and chopped, then heated through in the sauce at the last minute. They look pretty and taste delicious.

8 large scallops

4 thin slices of skinless salmon fillet, each weighing about 5 oz

3 shallots

6 cups watercress leaves

about 2 tablespoons dry vermouth

2 tablespoons low-fat crème fraîche

salt and freshly ground black pepper

1   Preheat the oven to 400°F. Pat the scallops dry with paper towels if necessary. Put the salmon slices between 2 sheets of cling film and flatten them with the bottom of a saucepan. Remove the cling film and cut each slice of salmon in half crosswise. Wrap each scallop in a slice of salmon, skinned side inwards.

2   Place the fish parcels seam-side down in a baking dish. Finely chop the shallots and scatter them over the fish. Pour in water to come halfway up the fish. Cover with foil and bake for 10 minutes. Meanwhile, chop the watercress, reserving a few sprigs for the garnish.

3   Remove the fish with a slotted spoon to a serving platter, cover, and keep warm. Strain the cooking liquid and make up to 2¼ cups with water. Pour into a saucepan, add 2 tablespoons vermouth, and boil until reduced by about half.

4   Lower the heat and add the watercress and crème fraîche. Heat through, stirring, then add seasoning to taste. If you like, add a splash more vermouth.

To Serve   Pour the sauce over the fish parcels and garnish with the reserved watercress. Serve immediately.

Serves 4

Preparation time: 15 minutes
Cooking time: 20 minutes

Chef's Tip

Fresh scallops are better than frozen for this recipe because frozen scallops tend to be watery after thawing. They must be absolutely fresh, so buy and cook them within 24 hours, keeping them in the refrigerator until you are ready to cook. To prepare scallops, pull off the tough crescent-shaped muscle on the side. This must be discarded because it is chewy and will spoil the finished dish.

◆

Variation

An aniseed liqueur such as Pernod can be used instead of vermouth.

BROCHETTES OF FISH WITH GINGER AND LIME

Three different types of fish provide contrasts of color, texture and flavor in these succulent broiled kebabs. The cooking juices are used to make an oriental-style sauce, which tastes delicious when served with fragrant Thai rice.

8–12 oz monkfish fillet

8–12 oz salmon fillet

8–12 oz cod fillet

2 limes

1 inch piece of fresh root ginger

3–4 tablespoons light soy sauce

freshly ground black pepper

lime wedges, to serve

Serves 4

Preparation time: 10 minutes, plus marinating time
Cooking time: 10 minutes

1   Skin all of the fish and cut it into even-sized cubes. Finely grate the lime rind and squeeze the juice. Peel and finely grate the ginger. Put the lime rind and juice in a non-metallic dish with the ginger and 2 tablespoons soy sauce. Stir together. Place the fish in the dish and stir gently, making sure that all the cubes are coated in marinade. Cover with cling film and marinate in the refrigerator for 1 hour.

2   Meanwhile, put 8 wooden skewers to soak in a bowl of warm water. Preheat the broiler.

3   Drain the skewers and thread the fish on them, alternating the different types. Place on the rack under the broiler and cook the fish for 4 minutes on each side.

4   Transfer the skewers to warm plates and keep hot. Pour the cooking juices into a small pan, add a few tablespoons of cold water and 1–2 tablespoons soy sauce to taste. Bring to the boil, stirring.

To Serve   Spoon the sauce over the brochettes, then grind black pepper over them. Serve with wedges of lime for squeezing.

Chef's Tips

It is quite tricky to skin fish without tearing the flesh, so buy the fish fillets ready skinned if possible. If you have to do it yourself, lay each fillet skin-side down and grip the tail end with your fingers dipped in salt. Cut between the fish and the skin at this end, then work the knife away from you using a sawing action at a low angle until you reach the other end of the fillet.

◆

If you keep root ginger in the freezer you will find it easier to grate when it is frozen hard than when it is fresh.

MOULES MARINIÈRE

This classic dish is naturally light and low in fat, yet not often thought of as such. Serve with a crusty baguette for mopping up the delicious juices. The quantities given here are enough for a first course for four people or a main course for two.

2 lb live mussels in their shells

1 onion

1 garlic clove

1 tablespoon olive oil

1 cup dry white wine

1 bay leaf

1 tablespoon fresh thyme leaves

2 tablespoons chopped fresh parsley

salt and freshly ground black pepper

Serves 4

Preparation time: 30 minutes
Cooking time: 10–15 minutes

Chef's Tip

Fresh mussels are normally available from the fall to spring. They are alive when you buy them, with their shells tight shut. Mussels that are open and do not close when tapped sharply should be discarded because they are not safe to eat – always buy slightly more than you need to allow for wastage. Frozen mussels are available all year round.

◆

Variation

Use dry Normandy cider instead of the white wine.

1   Rinse the mussels well in cold water and scrape off any barnacles with a small sharp knife. Pull off any hairy beards. Discard any mussels that are open or do not close when tapped sharply against the work surface. Give the closed mussels a final wash. Finely chop the onion and crush the garlic.

2   In a deep saucepan with a close-fitting lid, sweat the onion in the oil until softened. Add the garlic and stir for 1 minute, then add the wine, bay leaf, thyme, and drained mussels. Stir well, cover tightly and cook rapidly until the mussels have opened, about 5–10 minutes.

3   Remove from the heat and add the parsley and seasoning.

To Serve   Ladle the mussels and liquid into large bowls, discarding any mussels that have not opened. Serve immediately.

CLAM AND BLACK BEAN SALAD

Both clams and black beans are favorite ingredients and here they come together in this dramatic-looking salad which is full of flavor. Serve it with crusty French bread.

2 lb small live clams
⅔ cup dry white wine
2 garlic cloves
3 shallots
1 cup dried black beans, soaked in
   cold water overnight

4 large ripe tomatoes
1–2 tablespoons chopped fresh dill,
   to taste
salt and freshly ground black pepper

Serves 4–6

Preparation time: 40 minutes,
plus soaking time
Cooking time: about 1½ hours

1   Wash the clams in several changes of cold water and scrub them well. Discard any that are open or do not close when tapped sharply against the work surface. Pour cold water into a large saucepan to come about 1½ inches up the sides. Add the wine. Finely chop the garlic and shallots. Add the garlic and one-third of the shallots to the pan. Bring to a boil, tip in the clams, and cover the pan tightly. Cook over moderate heat for 10 minutes, shaking the pan often.

2   Tip the clams into a colander set over a bowl to catch the cooking liquid. Check that all the clams have opened, discarding any that are still closed. Remove most of the clams from their shells, reserving a few in their shells for the garnish.

3   Strain the cooking liquid through a muslin-lined sieve. Make up to 7 cups with cold water, return to the rinsed pan and bring to a boil. Drain the beans and add to the pan with half the remaining shallots. Boil hard for 10 minutes, then simmer until the beans are tender, 50–60 minutes. If necessary, top up with more water during cooking.

4   Halve, deseed, and dice the tomatoes. Drain the beans and mix them with the shelled clams, tomatoes, and remaining shallots. Add dill and seasoning to taste.

To Serve   Turn the salad into a serving bowl and garnish with the reserved clams in their shells. Serve at room temperature.

Chef's Tips

Use small clams, Little Necks or Cherrystones. These have sweet, tender flesh and are the most suitable varieties for salads. Soak them in a bowl of cold water for 2 hours before use. Clams are very sandy and this helps draw out the sand and make them less gritty.

◆

Black beans, sometimes called black turtle beans, have always been popular in Mexican and South American cuisines. They come from the same family as red kidney beans, but are slightly sweeter.

BOUILLABAISSE

A classic bouillabaisse is usually served with rouille (a chili-flavored mayonnaise) and croûtes made from fried or toasted bread. This simple version dispenses with these finishing touches and is therefore much lighter, but it tastes equally good.

10 oz monkfish

10 oz conger eel

10 oz red gurnard

10 oz cod

1 John Dory

10 oz sea bass

1 small leek

1 celery stick

1 small bulb of fennel

1 onion

2 garlic cloves

3 tablespoons olive oil

7½ cups fish stock

2 pinches of saffron threads

1 bouquet garni

salt and freshly ground black pepper

a few heaped tablespoons peeled
    and diced tomato, to serve

Serves 6

Preparation time: 20 minutes
Cooking time: 25–30 minutes

Chef's Tip

Bouillabaisse comes from the French port of Marseille in the Mediterranean, where it is made with many different kinds of locally caught fish. If the fish suggested here are hard to find, you can use any other white fish such as haddock, hake, sole, red snapper, sea bream, or whiting. Conger eel is an oily fish; mackerel or herring can be substituted for it.

1 Remove all skin and bones from the fish and cut the flesh into about 2 inch chunks. Thinly slice the leek and wash thoroughly. Thinly slice the celery and fennel, reserving the feathery tops for the garnish. Finely chop the onion and crush the garlic.

2 Heat the oil in a large saucepan and sweat the vegetables and garlic until soft, about 10 minutes. Add the stock, saffron, bouquet garni, and salt and pepper to taste, stir well and bring to a boil.

3 Lower the heat to a gentle simmer, then add the chunks of fish. Simmer until the fish is just cooked, about 10–15 minutes. Take care not to overcook the fish or it will fall apart.

To Serve Taste the soup for seasoning and ladle into warm soup plates. Top with the diced tomato and the reserved celery and fennel tops. Serve immediately.

BAKED FILLETS OF COD WITH A HERB CRUST

This is a very quick and easy dish, and it has the added bonus that it can be prepared several hours ahead of time, ready to pop in the oven when you need it. Serve with Braised Celery in Tomato Sauce (page 112) and new potatoes for a low-fat lunch or dinner.

1 tablespoon softened butter

1 shallot

2 garlic cloves

a few rosemary, thyme, and marjoram sprigs

a small handful of fresh parsley leaves

2 tablespoons olive oil

1 cup fine fresh white breadcrumbs

salt and freshly ground black pepper

4 pieces of cod fillet, each weighing about 6 oz

Serves 4

Preparation time: 20 minutes

Cooking time: 25 minutes

1 Preheat the oven to 350°F. Brush a baking dish with the butter. Chop the shallot and garlic. Strip the leaves off the herb sprigs and chop them finely. Chop the parsley finely, keeping it separate from the other herbs.

2 Heat the oil in a small skillet and sweat the shallot and garlic with the rosemary, thyme, and marjoram. Remove from the heat.

3 Put the breadcrumbs in a bowl with the parsley. Add the shallot mixture and mix well, then season generously with salt and pepper.

4 Season the fish, then press the breadcrumb and herb mixture all over it. Place it in the baking dish and sprinkle any remaining crumbs on top. Bake for 20 minutes or until the fish flakes easily with a fork and the crust is golden.

To Serve Place the fish on warm plates and serve immediately.

Chef's Tips

Make the breadcrumbs from stale bread in a food processor, working them until they are very fine, then spread them out on a tray and leave them to dry for a few hours — or overnight if possible.

◆

You can use fish with the skin on or skinless fillets, whichever type you find easiest to get. Cod is a soft, flaky-textured fish, which has a tendency to break easily. Cooking it with the skin on helps keep the fillets together.

◆

Variation

Haddock fillets may be used instead of cod.

Scrambled egg and smoked salmon tarts

These crisp little phyllo tarts make the most delicious brunch or lunch. The phyllo cases can be prepared a few hours ahead of time, so all you have to do is scramble the eggs just before serving.

2 tablespoons olive oil	salt and freshly ground black pepper	Serves 4
2 tablespoons butter	3½–5 oz thinly sliced smoked salmon	
2 shallots	8 eggs	Preparation time: 20–30 minutes
12 rectangular sheets of phyllo pastry (see Chef's Tip)	6 tablespoons low-fat milk	Cooking time: about 12 minutes

1   Preheat the oven to 375°F and put a large cookie sheet in the oven to heat at the same time. Brush the insides of four 4–5 inch tart pans lightly with oil. Melt half the butter in a small pan, then pour it into a bowl and mix in the remaining oil. Chop the shallots very finely.

2   Cut 24 disks out of the phyllo, about 1 inch larger than the pans. Brush 1 disk lightly with oil and butter and place it in a tart pan, tucking the phyllo into the inside edge. Brush another disk with oil and place on top of the first. Repeat with a third disk. Sprinkle with a quarter of the shallots, and salt and pepper to taste, then place 3 more disks on top, brushing the layers with oil and butter. Prick the base of the phyllo all over with a fork, then fill with crumpled foil. Repeat with the remaining 3 tart pans.

3   Put the pans on the hot cookie sheet and bake for 5 minutes. Remove the foil, return the pans to the oven, and bake for a further 2 minutes or until the pastry is golden brown. Set aside to cool a little in the pans. Cut the smoked salmon into thin ribbons. Beat the eggs with the milk and season well.

4   Melt the remaining butter in a non-stick pan and scramble the eggs over low heat for 3–4 minutes, stirring all the time with a wooden spoon. Stir off the heat for 1 minute.

To Serve   Transfer the phyllo cases to plates, then spoon in the scrambled egg and pile the smoked salmon on top. Serve immediately.

Chef's Tip

Phyllo pastry is available frozen in boxes at most supermarkets and Middle Eastern stores. Most boxes contain rectangular sheets in a roll, which must be thawed before they can be unrolled. Sizes vary according to manufacturer, so you may need more or less sheets than the number given here, which is based on the sheets being 12 x 7 inches. Phyllo pastry is very fragile and dries out very quickly when it is exposed to air. Always keep the pieces you are not actually working with covered with cling film or a damp cloth.

PAN-FRIED SCALLOPS WITH MANGO AND CHILI SALSA

Delicate scallops hardly need any cooking. In fact, the less you cook them the better – they can go rubbery and tough if overcooked. Serve this special dish for two with boiled white or saffron rice and a bottle of champagne or dry white wine.

6 large scallops

2 tablespoons olive oil

1 tablespoon unsalted butter

2 fresh cilantro sprigs, to serve

Salsa

2 large ripe plum tomatoes

1 small ripe mango

½–1 oz fresh cilantro leaves

1 large shallot

juice of 1 lime

¼ teaspoon Tabasco

salt and freshly ground black pepper

Serves 2

Preparation time: 20 minutes
Cooking time: 3–4 minutes

Chef's Tip

Scallops are usually sold off the shell at supermarkets and fish markets. Make sure they are fresh and have not been frozen and thawed, because frozen scallops tend to be watery and flabby. Before cooking, always pull off the tough muscle at the side of each scallop, but don't remove the orange coral if it is attached. The coral is a great delicacy – and it looks attractive too.

1   First make the salsa. Peel and dice the tomatoes. Peel, pit, and dice the mango. Chop the cilantro. Finely chop the shallot. Put all these ingredients in a bowl and add the lime juice, Tabasco, and salt and pepper to taste. Stir well to mix, then cover and chill in the refrigerator until ready to serve.

2   Pat the scallops dry with paper towels. Heat the oil in a non-stick skillet, add the butter, and stir until foaming. Add the scallops to the pan and cook for 3–4 minutes, turning them once until lightly golden on both sides and tender to the touch.

To Serve   Spoon the salsa on to 2 plates. Sit the scallops on top and garnish each serving with a sprig of cilantro. Serve immediately.

3

POULTRY, GAME, & MEAT

Meaty main courses often seem the most difficult when it comes to cooking light, but really it is only a question of choosing your cut of meat wisely and using the best cooking method for it. Animals are bred lean these days. Even pork, which once had a reputation for being a fatty meat, now has the minimum amount of fat. And venison, which you can now buy in supermarkets, is even lower in fat and cholesterol than chicken without its skin.

The rules are simple. For maximum interest and perfect nutritional balance, combine small amounts of meat with fresh fruit and vegetables. It tastes better and is better for you. Marinating works wonders with lean protein. It tenderizes fibers and injects flavor at the same time. Follow it up with a healthy cooking method like broiling, barbecuing, or chargrilling, and you've got the perfect complement to marinating. These two are close cousins when it comes to healthy cooking.

In this chapter you will find a variety of different birds and cuts of meat, none of which is difficult to get at the supermarket, but suggestions are given for alternatives which can also give more variety. There are recipes for everyday meals when you are in a rush after work, and recipes for dinner parties and other special occasions when you can cook at your leisure.

CHICKEN WITH SAGE AND LEMON EN PAPILLOTE

Fresh, light, and summery, this dish is very simple and quick to make. Serve it for a simple after-work supper, with new potatoes and a fresh green vegetable, or a mixed salad tossed in vinaigrette dressing.

4 skinless boneless chicken breasts

salt and freshly ground black pepper

2 tablespoons finely shredded fresh sage

grated rind and juice of 2 lemons

4 fresh sage sprigs, to serve

Serves 4

Preparation time: 20 minutes
Cooking time: 15 minutes

1   Preheat the oven to 400°F. Cut 4 pieces of foil, each about 12 inches square.

2   Place a chicken breast in the center of a square of foil and season generously with salt and pepper. Sprinkle one-quarter of the sage and lemon rind over the top, then drizzle with a little lemon juice. Wrap the foil around the chicken to make a parcel and fold over the edges to seal. Repeat with the remaining ingredients.

3   Place the chicken parcels on a cookie sheet and bake in the oven for 15 minutes, or until the chicken has cooked through. Unwrap a parcel and pierce one of the chicken breasts with a skewer – the juices should run clear, not pink or red.

To Serve   Unwrap the chicken and place on warm plates. Spoon the cooking juices over the chicken, drizzle with the remaining lemon juice, and garnish with fresh sage sprigs. Serve immediately.

Chef's Tips

Skinless boneless chicken breasts are easily available at supermarkets, ideal for quick evening meals after work. If you can get chicken breasts described as "part-boned" or "suprêmes," buy these instead. They are not as easy to find as boneless breasts, but they have juicier flesh, so are well worth seeking out.

◆

Foil measuring 12 inches wide is the best size for making papillotes.

◆

The parcels can be prepared the day before and kept in the refrigerator overnight. If you have the time, let them come to room temperature for about 30 minutes before putting them in the oven.

Turkey fillets poached in Madeira

The combination of ingredients in this recipe may seem unusual at first sight, but they give a truly delicious end result. Serve on a bed of plain boiled rice or noodles, and follow with a crisp green salad tossed in a mustard-flavored vinaigrette.

1¼ lb turkey breast fillet

1 cup ready-to-eat dried apricots

1¼ cups chicken stock

½ cup Madeira

grated rind of 1 orange

salt and freshly ground black pepper

2 teaspoons cornstarch

about 1 tablespoon chopped fresh cilantro, to serve

Serves 4

Preparation time: 10 minutes
Cooking time: about 20 minutes

Chef's Tips

Turkey fillet is naturally low in fat and cholesterol and there's no added fat in this recipe, which makes it exceptionally light. For convenience, buy turkey breast fillet that is already cut into strips. Most supermarkets sell it in packages, often labeled "turkey for stir-fries."

◆

Madeira is a fortified red wine from the Portuguese island of the same name. There are both sweet and dry varieties – the dry is most suited to savory dishes like this one. It is easy to find in wine stores and supermarkets, but you could also use a dry sherry, port, or vermouth, or a dry Italian Marsala wine.

1   Cut the turkey into strips. Halve the apricots lengthwise.

2   Heat the stock and Madeira in a sauté pan, add the apricots and orange rind, and bring to a boil. Add the turkey and stir well, then season generously with salt and pepper. Cover and simmer gently for 10–15 minutes until the turkey is tender, stirring occasionally.

3   Remove the turkey and apricots with a slotted spoon and keep them hot in a warm serving dish. In a small bowl, mix the cornstarch with 1 tablespoon cold water, then stir into the sauce. Bring to a boil and simmer for 2–3 minutes, stirring all the time until the sauce has thickened. Taste for seasoning.

To Serve   Pour the sauce over the turkey and sprinkle with the chopped cilantro. Serve immediately.

◆

Variation

Skinless boneless chicken breasts can be used instead of turkey.

QUAILS WITH ROAST BELL PEPPER SAUCE

Quail meat is tender, delicate, and low in fat, and it benefits from being served with a pungent-flavored sauce, as here. Rosemary also has a special affinity with quail, and is often cooked or served with it in the Mediterranean.

2 tablespoons clear honey

4 quails

a few fresh rosemary sprigs, to serve

Sauce

2 red bell peppers

a little olive oil

1 scant cup low-fat plain yogurt

salt and freshly ground black pepper

Serves 2

Preparation time: 20–30 minutes
Cooking time: 40–55 minutes

Chef's Tip

Quails are immensely popular along the Mediterranean coastlines of southern France and Italy, where you often see them spit-roasted on long metal skewers over open fires. Inexpensive farmed quail is now available all year round in supermarkets. Always serve 2 birds per person, because they are very tiny and do not have an abundance of flesh.

1   Make the sauce. Preheat the oven to 400°F. Halve the bell peppers lengthwise, and remove the cores and seeds. Lay the peppers skin-side up on a cookie sheet, brush with a little oil, and roast in the oven for 30–40 minutes, or until the skin has blackened and blistered. Remove the peppers from the oven, put them in a plastic bag, and leave to cool for 10–15 minutes. Leave the oven on.

2   Unwrap the peppers and peel off the skins. Place the flesh in a food processor or blender, add 4 tablespoons of cold water, and work to a purée. Turn the purée into a bowl, mix in the yogurt and add salt and pepper to taste. Cover and set aside.

3   Gently warm the honey in a small saucepan. Place the quails on a rack in a roasting pan, season, and brush with the warmed honey. Roast in the oven for 10–12 minutes, or until tender when pierced in the thickest part of a thigh with a skewer. Remove from the oven and leave to rest for 5 minutes.

To Serve   Arrange the quails on a warm platter and garnish with a few sprigs of rosemary. Hand the sauce separately.

SMOKED CHICKEN AND PAPAYA SALAD

This makes an excellent cold lunch in summer. Serve it very simply, with fresh crusty bread. It can also be served as a first course, in which case it will serve 6 people.

12 inch piece of cucumber

salt and freshly ground black pepper

2 ripe papayas

2 smoked chicken breasts, each weighing 6–7 oz

1 cos lettuce heart

Dressing

2 inch piece of fresh root ginger

3 tablespoons sunflower oil

2 tablespoons hazelnut oil

1 teaspoon white wine vinegar

1–2 teaspoons Dijon mustard, to taste

pinch of sugar

Serves 4

Preparation time: 15 minutes, plus standing time

Chef's Tip

A quick and easy way to remove cucumber seeds is to run a melon baller in a channel down the inside of the halved cucumber. If you haven't got a melon baller, use a sharp-edged teaspoon.

◆

Variation

Smoked duck can be used instead of smoked chicken, and mangoes instead of papayas.

1   Peel the cucumber, halve it lengthwise, and scoop out the seeds. Cut the flesh lengthwise in half again, then cut across these pieces to make small chunks of cucumber. Place in a colander, sprinkle generously with salt, and leave to stand for 30–60 minutes.

2   Rinse the cucumber thoroughly and pat dry. Peel, halve, and deseed the papayas, then cut the flesh lengthwise into neat slices. Remove the skin from the chicken breasts and cut the chicken lengthwise into slices of a similar size. Shred the lettuce heart.

3   Make the dressing. Peel and finely grate the ginger into a bowl, add the other ingredients, and whisk until well combined. Season to taste.

To Serve   Toss the lettuce and cucumber, then divide between 4 plates, heaping it up in the center. Arrange slices of chicken and papaya alternately on top and spoon the dressing over them. Leave to stand for 20–30 minutes for the flavors to mingle. Serve at room temperature.

GUINEA FOWL WITH A DRY SHERRY SAUCE

Both the guinea fowl and the richly reduced sauce have superb flavors in this simple recipe. Serve it in winter with Mash (page 187) and fresh vegetables. Brussels sprouts and chestnuts would be ideal.

6 oz shallots
1 tablespoon butter
1 tablespoon olive oil
4 guinea fowl breasts, each weighing
    4–6 oz
1¾ cups dry sherry

2¼ cups hot brown
    or chicken stock
salt and freshly ground black pepper
1–2 teaspoons chopped fresh flat-leaf
    parsley, to serve

Serves 4

Preparation time: 15 minutes
Cooking time: 20–25 minutes

1 Preheat the oven to 350°F. Thinly slice the shallots. Heat the butter and oil in a deep sauté pan and seal the guinea fowl breasts, skin-side down, for 4–5 minutes until golden brown.

2 Remove the breasts from the pan and place them, skin-side up, on the rack of a roasting pan. Finish cooking them in the oven for 10–15 minutes, or until tender when pierced with a skewer.

3 Meanwhile, add the shallots to the pan and cook over moderate heat for 5–7 minutes, stirring them frequently until they are golden brown. Remove with a slotted spoon and keep hot. Deglaze the pan with about three-quarters of the sherry, reducing it to a syrup. Add the stock to the pan and bring it to a boil, then boil rapidly until reduced by about half.

4 While the sauce is reducing, remove the guinea fowl from the oven and cover it with foil. Leave it to rest in a warm place.

5 Add the remaining sherry to the sauce and season to taste, then strain the liquid through a fine sieve into a clean pan. Cover and keep hot until ready to serve.

To Serve Slice the guinea fowl on the diagonal and arrange on warm plates. Place a few of the cooked shallots over the guinea fowl and sprinkle with chopped parsley, then spoon the sauce over and around. Serve immediately.

Chef's Tip

Guinea fowl is an excellent alternative to chicken because it has more flavor. Although strictly speaking it isn't a game bird, it tastes more like game than chicken, and is often sold in the game or specialist meat and poultry sections of large supermarkets. It is available all year round.

◆

Variation

Chicken suprêmes (breasts with the wing bone attached) may be substituted for the guinea fowl. If you find them difficult to slice, serve them whole.

ROAST CHICKEN WITH RED BELL PEPPERS AND TOMATOES

This dish is very easy to make, ideal in summer when the weather is warm and you have little inclination to cook. Bell peppers and tomatoes are ripe and flavorsome at this time of year too. Serve with a crisp green salad tossed in a herb vinaigrette.

1½ lb ripe plum tomatoes

3 large red bell peppers, total weight about 1 lb

4 garlic cloves

4 chicken pieces

2 tablespoons chopped fresh oregano

2 tablespoons olive oil

salt and freshly ground black pepper

Serves 4

Preparation time: 15 minutes
Cooking time: 40–50 minutes

1   Preheat the oven to 375°F. Halve, core, and deseed the tomatoes. Quarter the bell peppers lengthwise, then remove the cores and seeds. Thickly slice the garlic.

2   Slash the chicken with a sharp knife and place in a large non-stick roasting pan with the tomatoes, bell peppers, and garlic. Sprinkle with the oregano and oil, and season generously with salt and pepper.

3   Roast in the oven for 40–50 minutes, or until the chicken is cooked through. The juices should run clear, not pink or red, when the thickest part of the meat is pierced.

To Serve   Arrange the chicken pieces on warm plates with the roasted vegetables over and around. Serve hot.

Chef's Tips

Chicken quarters are best for this dish, either wings or legs. The skin of the chicken will help keep the flesh moist during roasting if you leave it on, but if you prefer less fat in the dish, remove it before cooking.

◆

Fresh oregano is not always easy to find, but you can use marjoram if this is easier to get. Oregano is a wild version of marjoram, with a slightly stronger taste. They are both used extensively in Mediterranean cooking and have a special affinity with bell peppers and tomatoes.

TURKEY WITH A CUCUMBER, CREAM, AND HERB SAUCE

Turkey is very low in fat and therefore has a tendency to be a dry meat unless it is cooked carefully. In this recipe it is poached gently in stock, a cooking method which helps make it moist and tasty. Serve with plain boiled rice.

½ cucumber

2 shallots

4 teaspoons olive oil

4 turkey steaks, each weighing 5–6 oz

2¼ cups chicken stock

salt and freshly ground black pepper

½ cup dry white wine

1 scant cup half-fat crème fraîche

1 tablespoon chopped fresh chives

1 tablespoon finely chopped fresh chervil

Serves 4

Preparation time: 10–15 minutes
Cooking time: about 20 minutes

Chef's Tips

For optimum flavor, use a homemade chicken stock (page 178) or one of the chilled fresh varieties sold in cartons at supermarkets.

Use scissors to chop the chives because they will cut through the delicate stems cleanly. If you use a knife to chop chives they can easily be crushed or bruised.

1   Peel the cucumber and cut it in half lengthwise, then scoop out the seeds and slice the flesh crosswise. Finely chop the shallots.

2   Heat 3 teaspoons of the oil in a sauté pan, add the turkey steaks, and cook for 1–2 minutes on each side until lightly colored. Add all but ½ cup of the stock and bring to a boil, then season to taste and simmer gently until the turkey is tender, 10–12 minutes.

3   Meanwhile, heat the remaining oil in a separate pan and fry the shallots over low heat for a few minutes until softened. Add the remaining stock and the wine, increase the heat and boil until reduced by half. Turn the heat down to low, add the cucumber, crème fraîche, and herbs, season well, and gently heat through.

To Serve   Lift the turkey steaks out of the stock and place them on warm plates. Spoon the sauce over and around and serve immediately.

POUSSINS WITH OREGANO, GARLIC, AND RED WINE

Young, tender-fleshed poussins (baby chickens) make a speedy, low-fat meal for any number of people. This recipe serves two, but the quantities of ingredients can easily be halved, doubled, or tripled. The timing remains the same.

4 garlic cloves

2 oven-ready poussins

1 small bunch of fresh oregano

salt and freshly ground black pepper

1 tablespoon olive oil

1¼ cups red wine

Serves 2

Preparation time: 20 minutes
Cooking time: 50 minutes

Chef's Tip

Poussins are four to six-week-old chickens, which weigh about 1 lb, just enough for one serving. Because they are young, the meat is very succulent — and much leaner than older chickens. They are up to 15% lower in fat and 10% lower in calories.

◆

Variation

If poussins are unavailable, use Cornish Rock Hens.

1   Preheat the oven to 350°F. Cut 2 garlic cloves into slivers and place inside the poussins with two-thirds of the oregano sprigs. Season the poussins with salt and pepper. Finely chop the remaining garlic and all but 4 of the oregano sprigs.

2   Heat the oil in a large casserole, add the poussins, and brown them gently, turning occasionally, until golden all over. Add the wine and enough cold water to come about halfway up the poussins, then sprinkle in the chopped garlic and oregano and bring the liquid to a boil. Quickly transfer the uncovered casserole to the oven.

3   Pot roast the poussins for 50 minutes, or until they are tender and sauce has reduced by about half. If the liquid reduces too much before the poussins are cooked, add a little extra water. When the poussins are cooked, remove them from the pan and place them on warm plates. Cover and leave in a warm place for about 5 minutes.

4   Spoon off any excess fat from the surface of the cooking liquid and bring the liquid to a boil on top of the stove. Boil rapidly until reduced further, stirring constantly, and loosening any cooking residue from the sides and bottom of the pan with a wooden spoon.

To Serve   Pour the sauce over the poussins, garnish with the remaining oregano sprigs, and serve immediately.

PARTRIDGE IN PHYLLO WITH A CARDAMOM SAUCE

Phyllo pastry is light because it is paper-thin and contains no fat. Here it is doubly useful because it protects the delicate flesh of partridge breasts during roasting. Celeriac Purée (page 188) is the traditional accompaniment for partridge.

8 boneless partridge breasts, each weighing about 2 oz

10 sheets of phyllo pastry

2–3 teaspoons olive oil

4 tablespoons mango chutney

2 tablespoons sherry or red wine vinegar

1¼ cups chicken stock

3 crushed cardamom pods

salt and freshly ground black pepper

Serves 4

Preparation time: 30 minutes, plus cooling time
Cooking time: 15 minutes

Chef's Tips

Fresh partridge is available in the winter months, from October onwards. It has a plump breast, so this is the best part of the bird to use. At other times of year, or if you can't get partridge, you can use pheasant, duck, or chicken breasts instead – allow 1 breast per person and remove the fat and skin before cooking. The flavor of the spiced cardamom sauce tastes good with any of these meats.

◆

To release the aromatic seeds of cardamom, crush the whole pods with a pestle or rolling pin or by pressing with your fist on the flat side of a large chef's knife. The pods can be left in the sauce because it is strained before use.

1   Preheat the oven to 400°F. Heat a non-stick skillet until hot and cook the partridge breasts for 2–3 minutes on each side until nicely colored. Remove from the pan and leave until cold.

2   Cut 8 phyllo sheets in half crosswise to make 16 pieces that are almost square. Brush a little oil on one of the pieces of phyllo, then place another piece directly on top. Place a partridge breast in the center and spread with 1 teaspoon mango chutney. Brush the edges of the phyllo with oil and wrap the phyllo around the partridge to make a neat parcel. Repeat to make 8 parcels in all.

3   Place the parcels on an oiled cookie sheet and brush the pastry with oil. Cut each remaining sheet of phyllo into quarters and scrunch each piece up with your fingers. Place on top of each parcel and brush with oil. Bake for 15 minutes or until the pastry is golden.

4   Meanwhile, deglaze the frying pan with the vinegar and add the remaining mango chutney, the stock, and cardamom pods. Simmer until syrupy and reduced by half. Strain and season.

To Serve   Arrange 2 phyllo parcels on each warm plate, drizzle the sauce over, and serve immediately.

STIR-FRIED GINGER CHICKEN

Low-fat protein and vegetables are combined in this fresh-tasting stir-fry, making this a quick and well-balanced meal for after work. Serve with boiled noodles or rice, which can be cooked at the same time as the chicken.

1 lb skinless boneless chicken breasts	extra soy sauce, to serve (optional)
2–2½ inch piece of fresh root ginger	
2 garlic cloves	*Marinade*
6 oz broccoli	2 teaspoons cornstarch
3 oz snow peas	1 egg white
1 bunch of scallions	2 tablespoons light soy sauce
2 tablespoons vegetable oil	1 tablespoon rice vinegar
2 tablespoons light soy sauce	
1 tablespoon rice vinegar	

Serves 4

Preparation time: 15–20 minutes
Cooking time: about 10 minutes

Chef's Tips

Most supermarkets sell chicken breast meat cut into strips ready for stir-frying. This will save you time if you are in a hurry.

◆

Any vegetable oil can be used for stir-frying, but groundnut (rapeseed) oil is one of the best because it is less likely to scorch when heated to a high temperature.

◆

Chinese rice vinegar comes in two different colors, red and white. The white is the stronger of the two and the most commonly available at supermarkets, but either color can be used in this recipe.

1   Cut the chicken into strips, about 1½ x ½ inch. Lightly whisk the ingredients for the marinade in a bowl, add the chicken, and stir well. Cover and set aside.

2   Peel and finely grate the ginger and crush the garlic. Divide the broccoli into tiny sprigs and trim the stalks. Cut the snow peas in half crosswise and cut the scallions into 2 inch lengths.

3   Heat the oil in a wok or deep sauté pan over moderate to high heat until very hot. Add the ginger and garlic and stir-fry for 1 minute. Add the chicken and stir-fry vigorously for 4–5 minutes, just until it turns white in color.

4   Add the vegetables, the soy sauce, vinegar, and 4 tablespoons cold water. Stir-fry for 2–3 minutes, or until the vegetables have softened slightly but still remain crisp.

To Serve   Taste the stir-fry and add more soy sauce if you like. Serve immediately.

THAI CHICKEN

Succulent skewered chicken that has been marinated in pungent Thai ingredients makes a delicious summer meal, served on a bed of fragrant jasmine rice. If you like, you can do the cooking on the barbecue rather than under the broiler.

4 cups fresh cilantro

2 garlic cloves

½ inch piece of fresh root ginger

½ bunch of scallions

1–2 green chilies, to taste

½ stalk of lemon grass

rind and juice of 2 limes

2 tablespoons light soy sauce

½ cup coconut milk

8 skinless boneless chicken thighs

lime wedges, to serve

Serves 4

Preparation time: 15–20 minutes, plus marinating time
Cooking time: 14–20 minutes

Chef's Tips

Coconut milk is an essential Thai ingredient, and cans and cartons are the most convenient way to buy it. The milk is made by steeping coconut flesh in water, then straining off the white liquid. When very thick, this liquid is called coconut cream or creamed coconut. Don't confuse coconut milk with the liquid inside a fresh coconut – this is not used in cooking but as a drink.

◆

Chicken thighs are excellent for marinating and grilling because the flesh is juicier than chicken breast, which tends to toughen when cooked by dry heat.

1 In a food processor or blender, finely chop the cilantro, garlic, ginger, scallions, chilies, lemon grass, and lime rind with the lime juice, soy sauce, and coconut milk.

2 Using a sharp knife, cut 3 diagonal slashes in each piece of chicken. Put the chicken in a non-metallic dish and pour the spiced mixture over them. Cover the dish with cling film and marinate in the refrigerator for several hours or overnight.

3 Preheat the broiler to hot. Thread 2 pieces of chicken on each of 4 metal skewers. Put the skewers on the broiler pan and broil for 7–10 minutes on each side, turning once.

4 Meanwhile, pour the remaining marinade into a saucepan. Bring to a boil and simmer for 5–10 minutes, stirring often.

To Serve Arrange the skewers on plates and spoon the cooked marinade over them. Serve hot, with lime wedges for squeezing.

LATTICE-CUT CHICKEN WITH HERBS

Mixed fresh herbs give chicken an intense flavor, and balsamic vinegar gives an exquisite boost at the last minute. Serve hot with new potatoes boiled in their skins and tossed in olive oil, or cold with Potato Salad with a Mustard Dressing (page 119).

1 small bunch of fresh chives or flat-leaf parsley

1 small bunch of fresh tarragon

leaves of 2 fresh rosemary sprigs

6 scallions

1 garlic clove

2 tablespoons olive oil

1 tablespoon tarragon vinegar

4 skinless boneless chicken breasts

4 teaspoons balsamic vinegar

Serves 4

Preparation time: 10 minutes, plus marinating time

Cooking time: 8–10 minutes

Chef's Tips

You can chop the herb mixture in a food processor. Strip the leaves off the rosemary and tarragon sprigs first, and use the pulse button so the herbs are not overprocessed.

◆

The chicken can be marinated for up to 24 hours. Cover the dish with cling film and refrigerate.

◆

While the chicken is cooking, press it down firmly with a fish slice or spatula so the ridges from the pan make charred stripes on the flesh.

1   Set aside a few herb sprigs for the garnish, then finely chop the remaining herbs with the scallions and garlic. Put half of the oil in a bowl, add the tarragon vinegar and chopped herbs, and stir together to form a thick herb paste.

2   Using a sharp knife, cut a criss-cross pattern in the smooth, rounded side of the chicken breasts. Put the chicken in a shallow dish and coat with the herb paste. Cover and leave to marinate in a cool place for at least 30 minutes.

3   Heat a ridged, cast-iron grill pan until very hot. Dip a wad of paper towels in oil and wipe it over the hot pan. Place the chicken on the pan and chargrill for 4–5 minutes on each side, or until the chicken has cooked through.

To Serve   Mix the remaining oil with the balsamic vinegar and drizzle over the hot chicken. Garnish with the reserved herb sprigs and serve hot or cold.

HONEY-BAKED CHICKEN

Sweet and tangy, these chicken pieces make really tasty hot or cold finger food for a party, and children love them. They are also good for an informal supper served with a saffron rice pilaf and a salad of crisp and colorful mixed leaves.

3 tablespoons clear or set honey

3 tablespoons Dijon mustard

1 tablespoon medium curry powder

8 chicken pieces

lime or lemon wedges, to serve

Serves 4

Preparation time: 10 minutes
Cooking time: 40–50 minutes

1   Preheat the oven to 350°F. Gently heat the honey, mustard, and curry powder in a saucepan until they have melted together and formed a paste.

2   Remove the skin from the chicken. With a sharp knife, slash the flesh right through to the bone. Put the chicken pieces in a non-stick roasting pan and pour the sauce over them. Turn to coat.

3   Bake the chicken for 40–50 minutes, or until cooked through and dark brown in color. Turn the pieces from time to time during baking, and add a few tablespoons of cold water to prevent the chicken from sticking to the pan and burning.

To Serve   Arrange the chicken pieces on a serving dish with the lime or lemon wedges. Serve hot or cold.

Chef's Tips

Dijon mustard is smooth and hot. If you prefer a milder flavor with texture use a grainy mustard, such as the French moutarde de Meaux.

◆

To get 8 neat pieces of chicken, buy 4 whole legs and cut them in half across their central joints to make 4 drumsticks and 4 thighs. If you are planning to serve the chicken as finger food, buy 8 drumsticks.

Pan-fried pigeon with a spiced plum sauce

Pigeon has a strong, gamy flavor and the breasts are plump and meaty, yet low in fat and cholesterol. The sauce in this dish is also highly flavored and quite spicy, so a plain accompaniment like boiled noodles or rice is called for.

2 teaspoons olive oil

8 pigeon breasts

2 tablespoons sherry vinegar

Plum Sauce

1 x 8 oz can plums in syrup

1 tablespoon clear or set honey

1 tablespoon dark soy sauce

1 teaspoon Worcestershire sauce

½ teaspoon Tabasco sauce

¼ teaspoon ground cardamom

salt and freshly ground black pepper

Serves 4

Preparation time: 15 minutes, plus chilling time

Cooking time: about 15 minutes

Variation

If you can't get pigeon, use duck breasts, which go well with the Chinese-style plum sauce. They are larger than pigeon breasts, so you will only need 2 to serve 4 people. Cut them in half on the diagonal and remove all the fat and skin before cooking.

1   First make the sauce. Put all the ingredients, except salt and pepper, in a small saucepan and bring to a boil over moderate heat. Simmer for 5 minutes, then remove from the heat and leave to cool.

2   Once the sauce has cooled, pour it into a food processor or blender and process until completely smooth. Check the seasoning, adding salt and pepper only if necessary, and transfer to a small bowl. Cover and chill in the refrigerator.

3   Heat the oil in a non-stick skillet and pan-fry the pigeon breasts for 3–4 minutes on each side until tender.

To Serve   Slice the pigeon breasts on the diagonal and arrange on warm plates. Quickly deglaze the pan with the vinegar and drizzle it over. Serve hot, with the chilled plum sauce handed separately.

CHARGRILLED CHICKEN WITH A FRUITY SALSA

The contrast of hot chargrilled chicken and cool refreshing salsa is a real taste sensation. Use as much chili as you dare to heighten the experience further. Prepare the salsa several hours ahead so that it gets really cold and the flavors mingle.

3 tablespoons olive oil

6 skinless boneless chicken breasts

juice of 1½ limes

4 fresh cilantro sprigs, to serve

Salsa

4 tomatoes

2 shallots

1 handful of fresh cilantro leaves

1–2 green chilies, to taste

1 mango

juice of 1 lime

salt and freshly ground black pepper

Serves 6

Preparation time: 20 minutes, plus chilling time

Cooking time: 10–15 minutes

Chef's Tips

There are many types of green chili. The small thin, pointed ones that are dark green in color tend to be fiery hot, while the fatter pale green ones are generally milder. If you like your salsa searingly hot, choose habañeros, bird's eye, or Scotch bonnet. Milder green chilies are anaheim, fresco, and jalapeño, but even these can be quite hot, so always use them with caution.

Mangoes have one of the most delicious flavors of all fruits when they are ripe and at their best, but they are so often spoiled by their stringy flesh. When shopping for mangoes, ask for Alfonso from India, or Sindri or Chaunca from Pakistan. These three varieties are among the sweetest and best for flavor, and their smooth juicy flesh literally melts in the mouth.

1   First make the salsa. Finely dice the tomatoes, removing the cores and seeds, and finely chop the shallots and cilantro. Cut the chilies lengthwise in half, scrape out the seeds, then dice the flesh very finely. Peel and pit the mango and cut the flesh into small dice. Mix all the ingredients in a bowl with the lime juice, and salt and pepper to taste. Cover and chill in the refrigerator until ready to serve.

2   Heat a ridged, cast-iron grill pan until very hot. Rub the chicken breasts with 2 tablespoons of the oil and season with black pepper. Place the chicken on the pan and chargrill for 10–15 minutes, or until cooked through, turning once.

3   Transfer the chicken to warm plates and season well. Add the remaining oil and the lime juice to the pan and stir vigorously with a wooden spoon to mix with any pan juices.

To Serve   Pour the juices over the chicken and garnish with cilantro sprigs. Serve immediately, with the salsa spooned alongside.

Cajun blackened chicken

Hot spices, herbs, pepper, and salt combine together to make a crusty coating for low-fat chicken breasts. Serve with boiled white rice and a cooling tomato salsa or a colorful tossed mixed salad.

4 skinless boneless chicken breasts
2 tablespoons olive oil
lime wedges, to serve

Spice Mixture
1 tablespoon cumin seeds
1 tablespoon dried oregano
1 tablespoon dried basil
½ tablespoon sea or rock salt
½ tablespoon garlic salt
1 tablespoon ground white pepper
1 tablespoon freshly ground black pepper
1 tablespoon cayenne pepper

Serves 4

Preparation time: 20 minutes
Cooking time: about 10 minutes

Chef's Tips

Cajun food is often cooked in butter to increase the blackened effect, but olive oil is used to here to keep the saturated fat content down.

The chicken can be left to marinate in the refrigerator for several hours, or overnight.

1   Make the spice mixture. Using a pestle and mortar, grind the cumin seeds to a powder with the oregano and basil. Mix with both kinds of salt and the three kinds of pepper.

2   Coat the chicken breasts with the spice mixture and set aside for at least 10–15 minutes.

3   Heat the oil in a non-stick skillet and pan-fry the chicken breasts for about 5 minutes on each side, or until cooked through.

To Serve   Arrange the chicken breasts on a warm serving dish with lime wedges for squeezing. Serve hot.

RABBIT IN A RICH TOMATO AND WINE SAUCE

This Italian-style recipe is similar to the classic chicken dish, pollo alla cacciatore, which is also made with tomatoes, wine, and rosemary. It is a hearty, warming casserole for a winter meal. Serve with crusty bread, polenta, or Mash (page 187) to mop up the juices.

8 skinless boneless rabbit joints

2 red onions

2 garlic cloves

10–12 fresh rosemary sprigs

2 tablespoons olive oil

salt and freshly ground black pepper

3 cups passata (sieved, pulped tomatoes)

1 tablespoon tomato paste

⅔ cup dry white wine

⅔ cup chicken stock

Serves 4

Preparation time: 20 minutes
Cooking time: 45 minutes

Chef's Tips

Skinless boneless rabbit joints are sold both fresh and frozen at most large supermarkets. They look and taste very similar to chicken but are slightly darker in color and stronger in flavor. If you prefer, this recipe can be made with skinless boneless chicken thighs instead of the rabbit.

◆

This is a good casserole to make the day before you need it because the flavors intensify if it is cooled down and then reheated. After cooling, chill it in the refrigerator overnight. When required, reheat it on top of the stove for 5–10 minutes until bubbling hot. If the sauce is too thick, add a little more stock, wine, or water.

1   Preheat the oven to 325°F. Cut the rabbit into large bite-size pieces. Slice the onions and crush the garlic. Strip the leaves from the rosemary sprigs and chop them finely.

2   Heat the oil in a flameproof casserole and gently fry the garlic with the rabbit pieces until golden brown. Add the onion and rosemary and cook for 2–3 minutes. Season generously.

3   Stir in the passata, tomato paste, wine, and stock. Bring to a simmer, stirring occasionally, then cover and cook in the oven for 45 minutes, or until the rabbit is tender.

To Serve   Taste for seasoning and serve hot, straight from the casserole.

VENISON STEAKS WITH A FRUIT SAUCE

Venison is a high-protein meat, lower in fat and cholesterol than beef and even skinless chicken, so it is a very good choice for a light diet. This is a dinner-party dish, which is quite rich in flavor. Serve it with plain seasonal vegetables.

2 shallots

4 venison steaks, each weighing about 5 oz

salt and freshly ground black pepper

¾ cup fresh redcurrants or cranberries

1 tablespoon olive oil

1¼ cups beef stock

4 tablespoons port

1½ tablespoons redcurrant jelly

4 fresh sage sprigs, to serve

Serves 4

Preparation time: 10 minutes
Cooking time: about 15 minutes

Chef's Tip

You can buy venison steaks at large supermarkets. Haunch steaks cut from the leg have lean, prime quality meat and are most reasonably priced. Because the meat is so low in fat, it is best to slightly undercook the steaks as here, then let the meat rest before carving and serving. This will prevent the meat drying out.

1   Finely chop the shallots. Season the steaks well with salt and pepper. Remove the redcurrants from their stalks, if using. Heat the oil in a non-stick sauté pan and cook the steaks over moderate heat for 3–5 minutes on each side, turning once.

2   Remove the steaks from the pan and set them aside to rest in a warm place. Lower the heat, add the shallots, and cook gently for a few minutes until softened and browned, then add the stock, port, and redcurrant jelly. Stir well, increase the heat and bring to a boil, then simmer until the sauce has reduced by almost half. Add the redcurrants and simmer until the sauce is syrupy.

To Serve   Carve the steaks into thin slices on the diagonal and arrange the slices overlapping on warm plates. Spoon the sauce over the steaks and garnish with the sage sprigs. Serve immediately.

Filet steaks with mushrooms and red wine

This is a classic steak served in true French style with an earthy mix of mushrooms and red wine. It is always popular with meat eaters. Serve with potato wedges (page 106) and a green salad tossed in Vinaigrette Dressing (page 184).

2 shallots

1 cup button mushrooms

2 teaspoons olive oil

2 filet steaks, each weighing 4–5 oz

salt and freshly ground black pepper

1 tablespoon red wine vinegar

½ cup red wine

4 tablespoons hot beef stock

Serves 2

Preparation time: 10 minutes
Cooking time: about 10 minutes

Chef's Tip

Filet steak has the least amount of fat of all the steaks. It is more expensive than sirloin, but there is no waste, it cooks very quickly and is beautifully tender – ideal if you are unused to cooking steak. For rare steak, cook for 2 minutes on each side; for medium, 3 minutes; for well-done, 4 minutes.

1   Heat a ridged, cast-iron grill pan until very hot. Meanwhile, thinly slice the shallots and mushrooms.

2   Dip a wad of paper towels in oil and wipe it over the hot pan. Place the steaks on the pan and chargrill for 2–4 minutes on each side, depending on how you like your steak done. Season the steaks with salt and pepper to taste, remove them from the pan, and leave them to rest on warm plates.

3   Heat the remaining oil in the pan, add the shallots and mushrooms, and stir for 3–5 minutes until the mushrooms are golden and juicy.

4   Add the vinegar and stir to deglaze the pan, then add the wine and simmer for a few minutes until the wine has reduced by about half and is syrupy. Remove the pan from the heat, add the stock, and stir to combine. Taste for seasoning.

To Serve   Spoon the mushrooms and sauce over and around the steaks and serve immediately.

VEAL WITH APPLE AND ONION WEDGES

Veal is lean and tender. Ingredients like vinegar, onion, and sharp
dessert apples give its delicate flavor a boost, and they are all very low
in fat. If you prefer, you can use slices of pork tenderloin, which is also
lean and low in fat.

4 veal escalopes, each weighing about ¼ lb

salt and freshly ground black pepper

1 red onion

2 red-skinned apples

a little olive oil

2 tablespoons white wine vinegar

⅔ cup dry white wine

⅔ cup chicken or vegetable stock

Serves 4

Preparation time: 10 minutes
Cooking time: about 10 minutes

Chef's Tips

*Veal escalopes are sometimes
called schnitzels. They are cut from
the filet end of the leg.*

*The best kinds of grill pan have
sides and are fairly deep, allowing
room to make a sauce in the pan
using the sediment and pan juices
with additional liquid, as instructed
here. If you have a flat grill without
sides, you can deglaze it with a
small amount of vinegar,
but then you will have to pour the
vinegar into a saucepan before
adding more liquid.*

1   Heat a ridged, cast-iron grill pan until very hot. Meanwhile,
season the escalopes with salt and pepper. Slice the onion. Quarter and
core the apples, leaving the skin on, then cut each quarter into three.

2   Dip a wad of paper towels in oil and wipe it over the hot pan.
Place the escalopes on the pan and chargrill for about 3 minutes on
each side, turning once. Remove from the heat and keep warm on a
serving platter.

3   Add the onion and apples to the pan and cook for 2 minutes on
each side, or until the onion has softened and the apple wedges are
tender with clear grill marks. Remove them from the pan, and place
over the veal. Keep warm.

4   Deglaze the pan with the vinegar, then add the wine and stock
and stir well. Simmer for about 5 minutes, or until the sauce has
reduced by about half. Add salt and pepper to taste.

To Serve   Spoon the sauce over the escalopes and serve immediately.

KOREAN BEEF WRAPS

These are based on the Korean speciality called bulgogi, sizzling spiced beef traditionally served with kim-chee, a spicy and sour pickled cabbage. Here the beef is wrapped in cool, crisp lettuce leaves with spoonfuls of sweet plum sauce.

1 lb sirloin steak	1 tablespoon dry sherry
a little olive oil	1 tablespoon rice vinegar
	1 teaspoon sugar
Marinade	
1 inch piece of fresh root ginger	*To Serve*
3 garlic cloves	iceberg lettuce leaves
1 mild green chili	plum sauce
2 tablespoons dark soy sauce	1 tablespoon toasted sesame seeds

Serves 4

Preparation time: 10–15 minutes, plus marinating time
Cooking time: about 10 minutes

Chef's Tips

To cut steak very thinly, wrap it in cling film and place it in the freezer for a few hours. When it is just frozen, you will find it much easier to slice than when fresh and soft.

To toast sesame seeds, dry-fry them in a non-stick skillet for a few minutes over low to moderate heat. Shake the skillet and keep the sesame seeds on the move to ensure they toast evenly and do not burn.

Plum sauce is sold in bottles in the oriental sections of supermarkets and at Chinese shops. Made from plums, sugar, vinegar, ginger, chilies, and salt, it is fruity and sweet with a spicy kick.

1   Make the marinade. Peel and grate the ginger and crush the garlic. Halve, deseed, and finely chop the chili. Put these ingredients in a large bowl and mix in the soy sauce, sherry, rice vinegar, and sugar.

2   Trim all the fat off the steak and cut the meat into thin strips, each measuring about 3 x ¾ inches. Place the strips in the marinade and mix well. Cover and marinate in the refrigerator for 3–4 hours, or overnight.

3   Separate, wash, and dry the lettuce leaves, then arrange them on a tray or platter, tearing or folding them into neat shapes and cupping them together if they seem thin. Fill 4 small bowls with plum sauce.

4   Heat a ridged, cast-iron grill pan until very hot. Dip a wad of paper towels in oil and wipe it over the hot pan. Place half the strips of beef on the pan and chargrill for about 5 minutes, turning them frequently with tongs. Remove the strips with tongs and keep warm while chargrilling the remainder.

To Serve   Put all the beef in a bowl and sprinkle with the sesame seeds. Let each person put a little plum sauce and a few beef strips on a lettuce leaf, roll up the leaf around them, and eat with the hands.

SLOW-COOKED LAMB

This is a wonderful winter casserole. The dried apricots dissolve into the sauce during cooking and create an intense, rich flavor. Serve with Mash (page 187) or crusty bread, and follow with a crisp green salad tossed in Vinaigrette Dressing (page 184).

10 baby onions or small shallots

1 large carrot or 2 small ones

2 celery sticks

2 garlic cloves

8 fresh sage sprigs

2 teaspoons juniper berries

1 tablespoon olive oil

about 2 lb shoulder of lamb, boned and cut into cubes

1 cup ready-to-eat dried apricots

1 cup red wine

about 3½ cups hot lamb stock

salt and freshly ground black pepper

Serves 4

Preparation time: 20 minutes
Cooking time: 2¼–2¾ hours

Chef's Tip

To get about 2 lb boneless lamb, buy a lean shoulder of lamb weighing about 3 lb and bone and cube it, removing as much surplus fat as possible. You can use the bones to make a brown stock, following the recipe on page 179.

◆

Variations

Boneless lamb neck filet can be used instead of shoulder. It is widely available at supermarkets. You will need about 1½ lb.

◆

Beef can be used instead of lamb. Buy 1½ lb boneless beef for stewing or casseroling. The cooking time will be the same as for the lamb.

1   Preheat the oven to 300°F. Peel the onions or shallots, leaving them whole and attached at the root end. Dice the carrot and celery. Finely chop the garlic and sage leaves, keeping them separate. Crush the juniper berries with a pestle and mortar.

2   In a flameproof casserole, heat the oil and quickly brown the lamb over moderate to high heat. Add the vegetables, garlic, juniper berries, and half the sage, then the apricots, wine, and about one-third of the stock. Season generously and bring to a boil.

3   Cover the casserole tightly with the lid, transfer to the oven, and cook for 2–2½ hours. Two or three times during cooking, spoon off any excess fat from the surface of the liquid, stir well, and add more stock. At the end of the cooking time, the lamb will be very tender and the liquid quite reduced.

To Serve   Taste and adjust the seasoning if necessary, then sprinkle with the remaining sage. Serve hot, straight from the casserole.

ORANGE AND ROSEMARY LAMB CUTLETS

The "eye" of the meat in lamb cutlets is very lean, tender, and juicy, but you need to take care to trim off as much visible fat as possible from around the meat and bones before cooking. Serve with new potatoes and a seasonal fresh vegetable.

2 racks of lamb

2 garlic cloves

2 teaspoons olive oil

grated rind and juice of 1 orange

2 tablespoons chopped fresh rosemary

salt and freshly ground black pepper

½ cup red wine

1 tablespoon redcurrant jelly

fresh rosemary sprigs, to garnish

Serves 4

Preparation time: 20 minutes
Cooking time: 20–30 minutes

Chef's Tip

Racks of lamb from the best end of neck usually have 6–9 bones in them. For 4 people you should buy 2 racks, so that each person will have at least 3 cutlets. Check with your butcher that he has removed the chine bone or you will find the rack difficult to carve. Your butcher should also trim and scrape the bones clean.

◆

Variations

If you like, you can thicken the sauce with 1 teaspoon cornstarch mixed to a paste with a little cold water. Add it while the sauce is being stirred and keep stirring to prevent lumps forming.

◆

Try serving the cutlets with Tangy Red Relish (page 182).

1   Preheat the oven to 400°F. Trim off as much fat as possible from the lamb. Chop the garlic very finely. Brush the meaty side of each lamb rack with 1 teaspoon oil, then press the garlic, orange rind, and rosemary on to the meat with your fingers and season generously with salt and pepper.

2   Place the lamb on a rack in a roasting pan and roast in the oven for 20–30 minutes, according to how well done you like your lamb. Transfer the lamb to a board and cover with foil to keep the meat warm and allow it to rest before carving.

3   Put the roasting pan on top of the stove and deglaze with the wine, then stir in the orange juice and redcurrant jelly. Bring to a boil and stir until the jelly has melted. Turn the heat down to very low.

To Serve   Carve the lamb into cutlets by inserting the knife between the bones. Arrange the cutlets on warm plates and spoon the sauce over them. Garnish with rosemary sprigs and serve immediately.

GRILLED MARINATED LAMB

This lamb is quite spicy hot from the chili and scallions, but the mint helps cool it down. Serve on a bed of rice with a side dish of plain yogurt or a simple tzatziki of yogurt mixed with chopped cucumber and fresh mint.

1 green chili
1 small bunch of fresh mint
1 garlic clove
½ bunch of scallions
rind and juice of 2 limes or 1 lemon
salt and freshly ground black pepper
1 lb lamb fillet, cut into large cubes
lime or lemon wedges, to serve

Serves 4

Preparation time: 10 minutes, plus marinating time
Cooking time: 8–10 minutes

1   Halve the chili lengthwise and remove the seeds, then finely chop the chili in a food processor with all but 4 tiny sprigs of mint, the garlic, scallions, and lime or lemon rind.

2   Turn the chopped mixture into a bowl, add the lime or lemon juice, and season generously with salt and pepper. Mix well. Add the lamb and thoroughly coat with the mixture, then cover the bowl with cling film and marinate in the refrigerator overnight.

3   Preheat the broiler to hot. Thread the cubes of lamb on to 8 small metal skewers and broil the lamb for 8–10 minutes, turning once.

To Serve   Arrange the skewers on plates with lime or lemon wedges for squeezing. Garnish with the remaining mint sprigs and serve immediately.

Chef's Tip

Buy lamb neck or leg filet. Neck is more juicy than leg, because it has a slight marbling of fat; leg is often so lean that it can be dry.

◆

Variations

Add ⅔ cup plain yogurt to the chopped mixture in the bowl before adding the lamb. Yogurt will help make the lamb more juicy, which is good if you are using very lean leg meat.

◆

For an alternative serving idea, remove the lamb from the skewers and stuff into warm pita pockets with a Greek-style salad of shredded crisp lettuce or white cabbage, sliced tomatoes, and cucumber.

PORK STEAKS WITH CIDER

Pork, cider, and apples indicate that this is a dish from Normandy, a region famous for these ingredients and a rich cuisine that uses them to the full. Cream is often used in Normandy too, but in this recipe the sauce is better without it.

4 pork steaks, each weighing about
    ¼ lb

1 tablespoon olive oil

12 small shallots

2–3 bay leaves

4 tablespoons cider vinegar

⅓ cup dry cider

2 large fresh thyme sprigs

salt and freshly ground black pepper

1¼ cups pork or chicken stock

1 teaspoon clear or thick honey

1 large Bramley apple

2 teaspoons cornstarch

fresh thyme sprigs, to serve

Serves 4

Preparation time: 10 minutes
Cooking time: about 45 minutes

1   Trim as much fat as possible off the pork. Heat the oil in a large flameproof casserole and add the pork, shallots, and bay leaves. Allow the pork to brown over high heat for 8–10 minutes, turning once.

2   Pour the vinegar and cider into the pan and stir well, then add the thyme and season well with salt and pepper. Add the stock and honey, bring to a boil and stir well, then reduce the heat to a gentle simmer. Cover and cook for about 30 minutes, or until the pork is tender when pierced with a skewer.

3   Meanwhile, quarter, core, and peel the apple, then cut into 1½ inch chunks. Add to the pork for the last 15 minutes.

4   Remove the meat from the pan and place on warm plates. Cover and keep warm. Mix the cornstarch to a paste with 1 tablespoon cold water, pour into the pan and boil for 1–2 minutes, stirring, until the sauce thickens. Taste for seasoning.

To Serve   Spoon the sauce over the pork, garnish with thyme and serve immediately.

Chef's Tips

Steaks cut from the leg or shoulder have no outer layer of fat or skin and are a good choice for this recipe. Shoulder is more moist than leg, but it is also fattier. Before buying, check there is only a light marbling of fat through the meat.

◆

Bottles of French dry cider from Normandy are sold at wine stores and some large supermarkets. Use some for the sauce and serve the rest of the bottle chilled with the meal. It is an excellent drink.

◆

Pork stock cubes are widely available at supermarkets, but if you don't want to buy them especially for this recipe, use chicken stock instead.

◆

If you can't get the pork steaks in the pan in a single layer, fry them in two batches in step 1.

PORK TENDERLOIN WITH TOMATO AND SAGE SAUCE

Rich, strong flavors are at the heart of the Italian-style sauce that coats slices of tender pork in this hearty, main course dish. Serve it in winter with polenta mash. In northern Italy, polenta and rich tomato sauces are traditionally served together.

1 onion	2 tablespoons olive oil
2 carrots	2 tablespoons red wine vinegar
2 celery sticks	⅔ cup red wine
2 garlic cloves	1 × 14 oz can chopped tomatoes
1 small bunch of fresh sage	1 tablespoon tomato paste
2 pork tenderloins,	salt and freshly ground black pepper
each weighing about ¾ lb	

Serves 6

Preparation time: 10–15 minutes
Cooking time: 35 minutes,
plus standing time

Chef's Tip

Pork tenderloin is an excellent meat for light cookery because it is very lean and tender. It is a prime cut from the centre of the loin – the pork equivalent of filet steak. Whole tenderloins are often sold at supermarkets in vacuum packs.

1   Finely chop the onion, carrots, celery, and garlic in a food processor. Finely chop the sage with a sharp knife, reserving some small whole sage leaves for the garnish.

2   Trim any fat and membrane from the pork and cut each tenderloin crosswise into 3 pieces. Heat the oil in a heavy-based, flameproof casserole, add the pork, and brown over moderate to high heat until well colored on all sides, about 10 minutes. Meanwhile, preheat the oven to 325°F.

3   Remove the pork from the pan and keep warm. Add the chopped vegetables to the oil in the pan, lower the heat and cook gently for about 5 minutes, stirring frequently until softened. Add the vinegar, wine, tomatoes, tomato paste, chopped sage, and salt and pepper to taste. Stir well to mix and bring to a boil, then return the pork to the pan and coat with the sauce.

4 Cover and bake in the oven for 15 minutes, turning the pork over and basting with the sauce halfway. Remove from the oven and leave to stand, without lifting the lid, for 10 minutes.

To Serve   Slice the pork on the diagonal and arrange overlapping slices on warm plates. Spoon the tomato sauce over the pork, garnish with the reserved sage leaves, and serve immediately.

4

VEGETABLES
& SALADS

The many different colors, textures and flavors of fresh
vegetables speak for themselves, which is why they are the absolute
favorite ingredients in light cooking. In many cases there is no
need to cook them at all. The raw vegetables are best just left as
they are. A freshly made dressing or a simple sauce is all that they
need. This saves time and energy, two very precious commodities.

In this chapter you will find a selection of vegetable side dishes
and vegetarian main courses, and some recipes that can double
as both. Vegetables are nothing if not versatile, and you will
quickly see how easy it is to plan meals around them without a
central theme of fish or meat. Many unusual and exotic vegetables
are included here to widen your repertoire and add interest to
your cooking. You will be surprised how easy these are to get,
and preparation and cooking are simpler than you think. The
combining of salad leaves with fruit is a delight, and a technique
you will return to again and again.

Nutritionists recommend that we eat five portions of fruit and
vegetables every day. We get vitamins and minerals from vegetables
and our bodies cannot store them – hence the need for a daily
supply. Fiber and carbohydrate are provided by some vegetables
too, and we also need these on a regular basis. For a healthy
balanced diet, vegetables and salads are a must.

Spinach, red onion, and raspberry salad

This colorful salad has a tangy sweet-and-sour dressing from the raspberries and vinegar. It goes well with plain grilled fish, meat, and poultry, and tastes especially good with grilled shrimp.

6 cups baby spinach leaves

2 oz frisée lettuce

2 red onions

½ cup raspberries

3 tablespoons red wine vinegar

2 tablespoons sunflower oil

about ½ teaspoon caster sugar

salt and freshly ground black pepper

Serves 4–6

Preparation time: 10 minutes

1   Wash and dry the spinach and frisée, then tear them in bite-size pieces into a bowl. Thinly slice the onions and add them to the bowl.

2   Purée two-thirds of the raspberries in a blender or food processor with the vinegar, oil, sugar, and a little salt and pepper. Taste for seasoning and add a little more sugar if the dressing is too sharp.

To Serve   Pour the dressing over the leaves and onions and sprinkle with the remaining whole raspberries. Serve within 2 hours.

Chef's Tip

Frisée is the French name for a slightly bitter tasting salad vegetable, which you may see labelled in English as curly endive. It is a member of the chicory family, hence its bitterness, but it has a loose, blousy head rather than the tightly furled cones which are normally associated with chicory. The leaves are ragged, with attractive frilly edges. It works well in this salad, its bitterness contrasting with the sweetness of the raspberries.

VEGETABLE CURRY WITH CUCUMBER RAITA

Serve this fresh-tasting curry as a side dish with a spicy Indian grilled chicken dish such as tandoori chicken or chicken tikka. It also makes an excellent vegetarian main course for two people served with rice, chapattis or naan, and mango chutney.

1 onion

2 tablespoons vegetable oil

1 cup diced carrots

1⅓ cups diced potato

1 tablespoon mild curry powder

pinch of chili powder (optional)

1½ cups diced zucchini

1 cup diced tomatoes

salt and freshly ground black pepper

2 tablespoons chopped fresh cilantro, to serve

Raita

½ cucumber

1 scant cup low-fat plain yogurt

Serves 4–6

Preparation time: 15 minutes
Cooking time: 30 minutes

Chef's Tip

If you can, buy an Indian brand of curry powder. There are very many different ones available, so experiment to find the one you like the best. Most are made with coriander, cumin, mustard, and fenugreek seeds, plus turmeric, peppercorns, and ginger – and varying amounts of dried red chilies. If you like a fragrant mix, look for ones that contain cinnamon, cloves, and nutmeg.

1   Thinly slice the onion. Heat the oil in a flameproof casserole until hot, then add the onion, carrots, potato, curry powder, and chili powder (if using). Stir-fry over low heat for 5 minutes.

2   Add the zucchini and tomatoes, 1 cup cold water, and salt and pepper to taste. Bring to a boil, stirring, then cover and simmer over low heat until the vegetables are tender, 20 minutes. Stir and check several times during cooking and add more water if the vegetables are dry.

3   Make the raita while the curry is cooking. Peel, deseed, and finely dice the cucumber and mix in a bowl with the yogurt, and salt and pepper to taste.

To Serve   Taste the curry for seasoning, transfer to a warm dish, and sprinkle the chopped cilantro over the top. Serve hot, with the bowl of raita alongside.

ROASTED FENNEL AND EGGPLANT

This is an easy vegetable dish for a dinner party because once it is in the oven it looks after itself. Serve it with something plain and simple like grilled or barbecued chicken or steak because the vegetables and flavorings are quite strong.

2 large fennel bulbs

10 oz baby eggplants or 1 large eggplant

2 garlic cloves

4 tablespoons olive oil

juice of 1 lemon

1 teaspoon fennel seeds

salt and freshly ground black pepper

2 tablespoons chopped fresh flat-leaf parsley, to serve

Serves 6

Preparation time: 10 minutes
Cooking time: 1 hour

1   Preheat the oven to 325°F. Remove any tough outer leaves from the fennel and cut each bulb lengthwise into about 6 sections. Remove the ends from the baby eggplants. If using a large eggplant, cut it into pieces roughly the same size as the fennel. Place the fennel and eggplants in a large, non-stick roasting pan.

2   Crush the garlic and mix it in a bowl with the oil, lemon juice, fennel seeds, and salt and pepper to taste. Pour this mixture over the vegetables, then stir to coat.

3   Roast in the oven for 1 hour, turning the vegetables several times.

To Serve   Turn into a warm vegetable dish and sprinkle with the parsley. Serve hot or at room temperature.

Chef's Tip

Baby egplants are in season during the summer. The most common variety has a beautiful glossy purple skin and is shaped like a very large egg, but you may also find pale lilac ones, some streaked with cream stripes, and even pure white, cream, and green ones, some of which are pear-shaped. Any of these can be used in this recipe, but the dark purple eggplants offer a better color contrast against the fennel.

◆

Variation

To add more color, add 1 large red bell pepper, cored, deseeded, and cut into chunks.

CRUNCHY BEANSPROUT AND MOOLI SALAD

Crunchy and spicy, this oriental salad makes a nutritious side dish to serve with plain grilled chicken, meat, or fish. For vegetarians it can be served with other salads, especially those made with grains.

½ lb mooli
3½ cups beansprouts

Dressing
2 tablespoons toasted sesame oil
1 tablespoon rice vinegar
½ teaspoon dried crushed chili flakes
salt

Serves 4

Preparation time: 10 minutes, plus chilling time

1   Peel the mooli, cut it into matchsticks, and place in a large bowl. Add the beansprouts and toss the two vegetables together.

2   Put the dressing ingredients in a screw-top jar with a pinch of salt and shake well. Pour over the vegetables and toss through. Cover and refrigerate until well chilled, about 4 hours.

To Serve   Taste the salad and add more salt if necessary, then turn into a serving bowl. Serve chilled.

Chef's Tips

Mooli is a Japanese long white radish, also called daikon, which is rich in vitamin C. It is sold in supermarkets and oriental stores. Look for baby mooli for this recipe. They are tender-crisp and sweet, perfect for raw salads.

◆

Beansprouts are sprouted mung beans. Nutritionally they are very good for you, containing protein, a wide variety of B vitamins, vitamin C, and amino acids. They are very low in calories.

◆

Variation

To further enhance the sesame flavor of this salad and to boost its nutritional content even further, sprinkle a handful of toasted sesame seeds on top as a garnish just before serving. Sesame seeds are rich in vitamins, minerals, calcium, iron, and protein.

BAKED BEETS WITH CHIVE DRESSING

The cooked beet that you buy often taste very vinegary and sharp, but if you cook it yourself it has a wonderful earthy flavor. Serve these whole beets as an accompaniment to chicken and pork, two meats that go especially well with beets.

8 fresh uncooked beets

Dressing
1 scant cup low-fat plain yogurt
3 tablespoons chopped fresh chives
1 teaspoon prepared mustard
salt and freshly ground black pepper

Serves 4

Preparation time: 10 minutes
Cooking time: 3 hours

Chef's Tip

Look for bunches of raw beets in supermarkets and stores. If you can only find cooked beets, check with the storekeeper – if he boils it himself and sells it freshly cooked, he may not display it uncooked. If you tell him that you need fresh beets for baking he will gladly sell it to you.

1   Preheat the oven to 300°F. Wash the beets, taking care not to split or tear the skins, then place them in a casserole. Cover tightly and bake in the oven for 3 hours or until the beets are tender when pierced with a fine skewer.

2   Whisk together the ingredients for the dressing, adding salt and pepper to taste.

3   Remove the beets from the casserole, cut a deep cross in the top of each one and open up the four quarters.

To Serve   Stand the beets on a warm serving dish and spoon the dressing into the center of each one. Grind black pepper liberally over the beets and and serve immediately.

WARM THREE GREEN SALAD

Broccoli, snow peas, and beans are bursting with vitamins and minerals, but so too are the sesame seeds which top them – and they contain protein too. Serve warm as a vegetable, cold as a salad. For a vegetarian main course, serve with rice or another grain.

1 head of broccoli

¼ lb snow peas

¼ lb fine green beans

salt and freshly ground black pepper

4 scallions

2 tablespoons toasted sesame seeds, to serve

Dressing

1 inch piece of fresh root ginger

1 garlic clove

5 tablespoons sunflower oil

3 tablespoons rice vinegar

Serves 4

Preparation time: 10–15 minutes

Cooking time: about 5 minutes

Chef's Tip

You can use the familiar kind of blue-green broccoli, called calabrese, which has tight, firm florets branching off a thick central stalk, or you can use sprouting broccoli, which is smaller and looser and often has purple heads. Chinese sprouting broccoli, available from oriental stores, is another choice, and it would go well with the Chinese flavorings in this dish.

1   First make the dressing. Peel and finely grate the ginger and crush the garlic. Place in a bowl and mix together with the back of a spoon to form a paste. Whisk in the oil and vinegar.

2   Cut the broccoli into small florets. Top and tail the snow peas and beans. Cook the broccoli in a saucepan of salted boiling water for 4 minutes, the peas and beans in a separate pan of salted boiling water for 2 minutes. Drain well and turn into a bowl.

3   Thinly slice the scallions on the diagonal, add to the vegetables and pour the dressing over the top. Add salt and pepper to taste and toss gently to mix.

To Serve   Turn the vegetables into a serving dish and sprinkle with the sesame seeds. Serve warm.

POTATO WEDGES WITH CHIVE AND YOGURT DRESSING

Served with a salad, these make an excellent vegetarian supper. They are also good for a buffet, arranged on a large plate with the dressing in a bowl in the center for dipping. The celery salt is an inspired flavoring – it makes the potatoes taste similar to parsnips.

4 large baking potatoes

3 tablespoons olive oil

1 teaspoon celery salt

½ teaspoon garlic salt

freshly ground black pepper

To Serve

coarse sea or rock salt

1 scant cup low-fat plain yogurt

1 bunch of fresh chives, chopped

Serves 4

Preparation time: 10 minutes
Cooking time: 45 minutes

Chef's Tips

Dry, floury potatoes are best for roasting and baking – you will often see them in supermarkets labelled simply "baking potatoes." If not, look for the following: Desirée, King Edward and red Duke of York. All of these have crisp skins and soft, fluffy flesh when roasted or baked.

◆

Without the yogurt and chive dressing, the potato wedges make an excellent low-fat alternative to roast potatoes. This quantity should serve 6 people.

1   Preheat the oven to 400°F. Scrub the potatoes, then cut each one lengthwise into 6 pieces. Put the wedges in a large non-stick roasting pan, add the oil and toss to coat. Mix together the celery and garlic salts and plenty of pepper, then sprinkle over the potato wedges.

2   Roast the potatoes in the oven for 45 minutes or until crisp and golden, turning them several times to ensure even cooking. Meanwhile, put the yogurt in a bowl, add most of the chives and season well. Stir well to mix.

To Serve   Turn the potato wedges into a warm bowl and sprinkle with sea or rock salt to taste. Spoon the yogurt into a small serving bowl and sprinkle the remaining chives over the top. Serve immediately.

Chard, arugula, and radish salad

The contrasting colors of this salad make it really eye-catching, and the flavors of the leaves and the orange dressing go well together. It is good with chargrilled, broiled, or barbecued meat, especially steak, lamb chops, and chicken breasts.

4 cups baby spinach leaves

4 cups red chard leaves

4 cups arugula leaves

3 oz radishes

Dressing

juice of 1 orange

1 teaspoon coarsegrain mustard

3 tablespoons extra virgin olive oil

salt and freshly ground black pepper

Serves 4

Preparation time: 10–15 minutes

Chef's Tip

Red chard, also called ruby chard and rhubarb chard, has small green leaves like baby spinach, but it takes its name from its scarlet stems and veins, which make it look very pretty. Its leaves are very similar to spinach beet, which are actually the tops of a type of beet grown specifically for its leaves. You will find bags of red chard in supermarkets – it is in season in the summer months.

1   First make the dressing. Whisk the orange juice in a large bowl with the mustard, oil, and salt and pepper to taste.

2   Wash and drain the salad leaves. Spin them in a salad spinner or dry them with a clean cloth. Tear the spinach into bite-size pieces if the leaves are large. Slice the radishes very thinly.

3   Add the salad leaves and radishes to the bowl of dressing and toss well until the leaves are evenly coated.

To Serve   Transfer the salad to a serving bowl and serve immediately.

HONEY-ROASTED PUMPKIN AND SWEET POTATO

This makes a good vegetable dish in the fall, when there is a wide variety of different pumpkins and squash available. Sweet potatoes are a great alternative to ordinary roast potatoes, because they have more color and flavor.

about 1½ lb pumpkin

2 sweet potatoes

2 tablespoons olive oil

1 tablespoon clear honey

1–2 teaspoons Cajun spice, to taste

salt and freshly ground black pepper

Serves 4

Preparation time: 10 minutes

Cooking time: 1 hour

1   Preheat the oven to 350°F. Cut the pumpkin into wedges and remove the peel, seeds, and fibers. Peel the sweet potatoes and cut them into similar-size pieces.

2   Put the pumpkin and sweet potatoes in a large non-stick roasting pan and drizzle the oil and honey over them. Sprinkle with the spice and season generously with salt and pepper.

3   Roast in the oven for 1 hour or until golden and tender, turning and basting occasionally,

To Serve   Turn into a warm serving dish and serve immediately.

Chef's Tips

Pumpkins grow to enormous sizes, but they are often sold by the piece, so you can buy as much as you need. For a change, you could also use a fall or winter squash, such as butternut.

You can buy jars of ground Cajun spice, or make your own spice mixture according to the recipe given in Cajun Blackened Chicken (page 82).

SPICED AVOCADO AND STRAWBERRY SALAD

Avocados and strawberries make a stunning salad, and balsamic vinegar dressing is a classic with strawberries in Italy. Serve this salad for a summer barbecue party – it looks and tastes sensational.

2 cups ripe strawberries

2 large avocados, not too ripe

½ small iceberg or cos lettuce

Dressing

1 teaspoon Sichuan peppercorns

2 tablespoons balsamic vinegar

1 teaspoon caster sugar

Serves 6–8

Preparation time: 10–15 minutes, plus standing time

Chef's Tips

This salad tastes very good with barbecued food, especially chicken, but it also goes well with goat cheese and soft cheeses like fromage blanc and cottage cheese.

◆

Avocados are a healthy choice, eaten in moderation. They are rich in vitamins and minerals and they do not contain any cholesterol. Half an avocado contains about the same amount of calories as a handful of dry roasted nuts.

1   First make the dressing. Crush the peppercorns with a pestle and mortar or the end of a rolling pin, then mix in a small bowl with the vinegar and sugar.

2   Cut the strawberries into halves (or quarters if they are very large) and place them in a large bowl. Halve, peel, and pit the avocados. Slice the flesh into wedges and add to the strawberries.

3   Pour the dressing over the strawberries and avocados, turn very gently to coat, then cover and leave to stand for 30 minutes.

To Serve   Separate the lettuce leaves and use to line a shallow serving dish. Spoon the avocados and strawberries in the center. Serve as soon as possible, at room temperature.

BRAISED CELERY IN TOMATO SAUCE

Celery is often overlooked as a vegetable and used only raw in salads, but it has an excellent flavor when cooked and served hot, and it is very low in calories. This dish is good served with broiled or roast lamb or chicken, or with broiled or chargrilled steak.

3 celery hearts, total weight about 1 lb

2 shallots

2 garlic cloves

2 tablespoons olive oil

2 x 14 oz cans chopped tomatoes

1 tablespoon chopped fresh thyme

1 tablespoon chopped fresh oregano

salt and freshly ground black pepper

Serves 6

Preparation time: 10 minutes
Cooking time: 25–30 minutes

Chef's Tips

You can buy packs of celery hearts in supermarkets. They are the pale, tender central stalks of celery heads.

◆

A wide, deep sauté pan is ideal for cooking the celery and tomatoes, but if you haven't got one, use a wok with a lid.

◆

Variation

This recipe works equally well with fennel instead of the celery hearts, and marjoram instead of the oregano. If you can't get fresh herbs in winter, use 1 teaspoon each dried. Fresh plum tomatoes can be used in the summer. You will need about 1½ lb.

1   Cut each celery heart into 6 lengthwise, retaining a little root at the end to keep each section together. Wash well and drain. Finely chop the shallots and crush the garlic.

2   Heat the oil in a sauté pan and cook the shallots over low heat for 2–3 minutes without coloring. Add the celery in a single layer, then add the tomatoes, garlic, and chopped herbs. Season with salt and pepper and bring to a boil.

3   Cover the pan, lower the heat, and simmer for about 20 minutes or until the celery is tender. If the liquid reduces down and becomes too thick during cooking, add a few tablespoons of cold water.

To Serve   Taste the sauce for seasoning. Turn the celery and sauce into a warm serving dish. Serve hot.

CHARGRILLED BELL PEPPERS AND SWEET POTATOES

Using a ridged cast-iron pan for chargrilling vegetables is an excellent way to keep fat content down because you only need the smallest amount of oil and yet the flavor is superb. Serve as a side dish, with your favorite broiled meat or fish.

2 red bell peppers
2 yellow bell peppers
2 green bell peppers
1 sweet potato
1–2 tablespoons olive oil

Dressing
1 teaspoon cumin seeds
2 teaspoons clear honey
2 tablespoons balsamic vinegar
1 tablespoon walnut oil
1 tablespoon extra virgin olive oil
salt and freshly ground black pepper

Serves 4–6

Preparation time: 20 minutes
Cooking time: 25–30 minutes

Chef's Tip

The cumin seeds are dry-fried to help release their flavor. If you like, you can crush them with a pestle and mortar after dry-frying.

◆

Variation

Other vegetables, such as sliced zucchini, fennel, and eggplants, can be cooked in the same way. Allow 8–10 minutes cooking time for each, turning once.

1   Halve the peppers lengthwise and discard the stalks, cores, and seeds. Cut each half lengthwise into 4 pieces. Peel the sweet potato and slice it into rings about ¼ inch thick.

2   Make the dressing. In a small non-stick skillet, dry-fry the cumin seeds over low heat for a few minutes, taking care not to burn them. Place them in a bowl with the honey, vinegar, and oils, and whisk together. Season with salt and pepper.

3   Heat a ridged, cast-iron grill pan until very hot. Place the sweet potato slices on the pan and lightly brush each piece with olive oil. Cook for about 10 minutes, turning the pieces over once, then remove them from the pan and keep warm.

4   Add half the pepper pieces, brush with olive oil, and cook for about 8 minutes, turning them over several times. Remove and add to the sweet potatoes, then repeat with the remaining peppers, adding more olive oil if you need it.

To Serve   Place the vegetables on a large shallow dish and drizzle the dressing over them. Serve warm.

SALAD NIÇOISE

This must be one of the best salads ever. The combination of ingredients is just perfect, and it is impossible to eat it without thinking of the Provençal sun. Serve for an al fresco lunch with a crusty baguette.

½ lb small new or salad potatoes

salt and freshly ground black pepper

½ lb fine green beans

1 head of round lettuce

6 cups arugula leaves

12 cherry tomatoes

12 black olives

12 hard-boiled quail eggs

1 onion

1 x 7 oz can tuna in spring water
  or brine

Vinaigrette

⅓ cup extra virgin olive oil

3 tablespoons white wine vinegar

Serves 4

Preparation time: 20 minutes

Cooking time: 20–25 minutes

Chef's Tips

Use small potatoes for salads such as German yellow fingerlings and yukon gold. They have waxy yellow flesh which stays in shape when they are sliced after boiling, and they both have a very good flavor. They are widely available in supermarkets.

◆

Extra virgin olive oil is from the first cold pressing of the olives. It is the most expensive of the olive oils, but it is worth buying as good a bottle as you can afford to keep for salads like this one. Olive oil from Provence would be particularly appropriate here, but Italian, Greek, and Spanish olive oils are all good, and you should buy according to the color and flavor you like the most.

1   Put the potatoes in a saucepan of salted boiling water, bring back to a boil, and cook for 20–25 minutes until just tender. Meanwhile, top and tail the beans and slice them diagonally in half. Bring another pan of water to a boil, add a pinch of salt and then the beans. Cook for about 5 minutes until just tender.

2   Drain the potatoes and beans well. Cut the potatoes into halves or quarters, depending on their size. Make the vinaigrette. Whisk the oil and vinegar together in a jug with salt and pepper to taste. Gently toss the potatoes and beans in half the vinaigrette.

3   Separate the lettuce leaves and wash and dry them with the arugula. Halve the tomatoes, and halve and pit the olives. Shell and halve the quail eggs. Slice the onion into thin rings. Drain the tuna and break it into large bite-size flakes.

To Serve   Divide the salad leaves between 4 plates and top with the potatoes and beans followed by the remaining ingredients and vinaigrette. Grind pepper over the salad and serve.

MIXED MUSHROOM RAGOÛT

This ragoût is like a vegetarian stroganoff – the mushrooms are so full of flavor and substance that it tastes almost meaty. It can be served as a main course on a bed of boiled or steamed rice, or on its own as a vegetable side dish.

1 onion

about 1 lb mixed mushrooms

2 tablespoons butter

⅓ cup vegetable stock

1 tablespoon Madeira

2 tablespoons chopped fresh thyme

salt and freshly ground black pepper

To Serve

2 tablespoons low-fat crème fraîche

1–2 tablespoons chopped fresh parsley

Serves 4–6

Preparation time: 10 minutes
Cooking time: 15 minutes

Chef's Tips

You can buy inexpensive packs of mixed mushrooms at supermarkets. The contents of the packs vary and some contain wild and cultivated mixed together – these are often labelled "exotic." For this dish you can use any variety you like, such as shiitake, chestnut, portobello, girolles, and ceps.

◆

Madeira is a strong, fortified red wine from the island of the same name. Even the small amount used here gives a wonderful depth of flavor to the mushrooms. If you do not have Madeira, you can use port, sherry, or brandy instead.

◆

Variation

Add 1–2 garlic cloves, crushed, with the mushrooms in step 2.

1   Slice the onion very finely, then slice the mushrooms so they are about the same size as the onion slices but slightly thicker. Melt the butter in a sauté pan, add the onion, and cook over low heat for about 5 minutes until soft but not colored.

2   Add the mushrooms, stir well and cook for 5 minutes. Add the stock and Madeira, cover and simmer gently for about 5 minutes or until the mushrooms are tender. Remove from the heat, add half the thyme, and season generously with salt and pepper.

To Serve   Swirl the crème fraîche into the mushrooms and turn into a warm dish. Mix the remaining thyme with the parsley, sprinkle over the mushrooms and serve immediately.

SPINACH AND GOAT CHEESE ROULADE

The combination of spinach and goat cheese is hard to beat in a roulade, and this one can be served warm or at room temperature. It makes a delicious lunch dish served with Tangy Red Relish (page 182) and a crusty baguette.

1 cup frozen leaf spinach, thawed and drained

¼ cup flour

¼–½ teaspoon freshly grated nutmeg, to taste

2 tablespoons chopped fresh chives

salt and freshly ground black pepper

3 eggs, separated

Filling

½ cup soft goat cheese

1 scant cup half-fat crème fraîche

1¼ cups peeled, diced cucumber

Serves 4–6

Preparation time: 20–30 minutes
Cooking time: 20 minutes

Chef's Tip

Frozen spinach is convenient and it saves time, but if you want to use fresh spinach you will need 1 lb. Wash it well and place it in a large saucepan with only the water that clings to the leaves. Cover and cook over low to moderate heat for 5 minutes or until wilted and tender. Drain thoroughly before use.

1   Preheat the oven to 350°F and line a 13 x 9 inch jelly-roll pan with non-stick baking parchment.

2   Squeeze as much moisture as possible from the spinach, then put the spinach in a food processor with the flour, nutmeg, chives, and plenty of salt and pepper. Process until almost smooth, then turn into a large bowl. Add the egg yolks and beat well to mix.

3   In a separate clean bowl, whisk the egg whites with a pinch of salt until firm. Fold into the spinach, then spread evenly in the pan. Bake for 20 minutes or until firm. Turn out the roulade onto a clean sheet of baking parchment on a wire rack and leave to cool.

4   Mix the goat cheese and crème fraîche in a bowl and season well. Stir the cucumber into the cheese mixture. When the roulade is completely cool, spread it with the cheese mixture, and roll up from one long edge into a roulade, using the parchment paper to help support it.

To Serve   Cut the roulade crosswise into 8 slices. Arrange the slices slightly overlapping on a warm serving dish and serve immediately.

POTATO SALAD WITH A MUSTARD DRESSING

Using low-fat mayonnaise and yogurt gives a light and tangy taste to potato salad, making it far less rich than the classic recipe. The mustard and chives accentuate the tanginess and make it good to serve with cold meats, smoked fish, or frankfurters.

2 lb waxy new potatoes

salt and freshly ground black pepper

½ cup low-fat natural yogurt

3 tablespoons low-fat or light mayonnaise

1 tablespoon coarsegrain mustard

1 small bunch of fresh chives

Serves 4–6

Preparation time: 10 minutes

Cooking time: 25–30 minutes

Chef's Tips

Try to use the smallest new potatoes you can find because this salad looks most attractive when made with whole potatoes. Many supermarkets sell baby new potatoes, which are about the same size as cherry tomatoes. If you can't get these, cut the potatoes into halves, quarters, or slices after cooking and cooling.

The salad can be prepared several hours ahead and kept covered in the refrigerator. Let it come to room temperature about 30 minutes before serving.

1   Put the potatoes in a saucepan of salted boiling water, bring back to a boil and cook for 20–25 minutes until just tender. Drain the potatoes and plunge into a bowl of iced water for 5 minutes to stop them cooking. Drain well and leave to cool.

2   Mix the yogurt, mayonnaise, and mustard together in a large bowl and season generously with salt and pepper. Add the potatoes. Using scissors, snip most of the chives over the potatoes. Fold the potatoes in the dressing until evenly coated, then taste for seasoning.

To Serve   Transfer the salad to a serving bowl and garnish with the remaining chives, either snipped or as whole stems. If you like, grind black pepper liberally over the top.

RED AND GREEN SALAD

Sweet and tangy with a hint of fresh mint, this stunning salad makes a good accompaniment for roast lamb, broiled lamb chops and cutlets, or barbecued kebabs. It also goes well with cheese.

5 oz sugarsnap peas or snow peas

salt and freshly ground black pepper

4 cups torn red chard leaves

4 cups torn radicchio leaves

Dressing

grated rind and juice of ½ lemon

2 tablespoons extra virgin olive oil

1 tablespoon chopped fresh mint

2 teaspoons clear honey

Serves 4–6

Preparation time: 15 minutes
Cooking time: 2 minutes

Chef's Tips

Sugarsnap peas are plumper and rounder than snow peas, which tend to be completely flat in shape, but otherwise they are very similar to one another and can be used interchangeably.

◆

Red chard is a beautiful salad vegetable with dainty, tender green leaves, bright red stems and a mild flavor. It is a variety of Swiss chard, which comes from the same family as beet, and is sometimes called ruby chard or rhubarb chard. If you can't get red chard on its own, look for it in bags of ready prepared "continental" salad at supermarkets. It is often combined with lollo rosso, red leaf lettuce, and arugula, all of which would be suitable for this salad.

1   Top and tail the peas and simmer in salted boiling water until just tender but still al dente, about 2 minutes. Drain into a colander and rinse under the cold tap until completely cold. Pat dry, then cut crosswise into halves or thirds, depending on their size.

2   Tear the chard and radicchio leaves into bite-size pieces and place in a large bowl. Add the peas and toss with your hands until the vegetables are evenly combined.

3   Make the dressing. In a small jug, whisk the lemon rind and juice with the oil, mint, honey, and salt and pepper to taste. Pour the dressing over the peas and leaves and toss to mix.

To Serve   Turn into a salad bowl and serve immediately.

SHREDDED SPROUTS AND WATER CHESTNUTS

Except at Christmas, sprouts are often overlooked as a vegetable, but they deserve to be eaten more often because they are a good source of vitamins and minerals. Serve as a side dish, or as a vegetarian main course for two with Thin Egg Pancakes (page 189).

2 shallots

½ lb Brussels sprouts

1 x 8 oz can water chestnuts

2 scallions

2 tablespoons sunflower oil

1 tablespoon dark soy sauce

salt and freshly ground black pepper

Serves 4

Preparation time: 10–15 minutes
Cooking time: 10 minutes

Variations

When fresh sprouts are out of season, use frozen button sprouts. Thaw them, then cut each one lengthwise in half. They will take 5 minutes to cook in step 2.

Increase the heat and the oriental flavor of this dish by adding 1 red-hot fresh chili, deseeded and finely chopped, with the shallots.

1   Chop the shallots. Remove the outer leaves from the sprouts if necessary, then slice the sprouts into very thin ribbons. Drain the water chestnuts and slice each one lengthwise into three. Thinly slice the scallions on the diagonal.

2   Heat the oil in a large non-stick skillet and sweat the shallots over low heat for about 5 minutes until soft. Add the sprouts, increase the heat, and stir-fry for a few minutes until tinged golden brown.

3   Add the water chestnuts, scallions, and soy sauce and heat through, stirring, then taste and add salt and pepper if necessary.

To Serve   Turn into a warm dish and serve immediately.

SCALLION CRÊPES WITH CHARGRILLED ASPARAGUS

Crêpes made with half vegetable stock and half milk are lighter than those made with all milk, and the fromage frais filling spiked with paprika and orange is also light. Serve for a vegetarian lunch or supper with a crusty baguette or ciabatta.

2 scallions
crêpe batter (page 171)
1–2 tablespoons olive oil
salt and freshly ground black pepper
1 scant cup fromage frais

1 teaspoon paprika
½ teaspoon grated orange rind
12 young tender asparagus spears
a little extra paprika, for dusting

Serves 4

Preparation time: 25 minutes, plus standing time
Cooking time: 20 minutes

1   Thinly slice the scallions and add to the crêpe batter with 1 tablespoon oil, and salt and pepper to taste. Mix together the fromage frais, paprika, and orange rind in a small bowl until smooth. Season to taste.

2   Make 8 crêpes with the batter according to the instructions on page 171, stacking the crêpes on top of each other as they are done (this will keep them warm).

3   Heat a ridged, cast-iron grill pan until very hot. Cut each asparagus spear crosswise in half. Dip a wad of paper towels in oil and wipe it over the hot pan. Place the asparagus on the pan and chargrill for 5–8 minutes or until tender, turning once. Remove from the heat.

4   Spread 1 crêpe with one-eighth of the fromage frais mixture, fold in half, then in half again to make a fan shape. Tuck the asparagus inside, allowing the tips to peep out. Repeat with the remaining crêpes, filling, and asparagus.

To Serve   Place 2 crêpes on each plate and dust very lightly with paprika. Serve immediately.

Variation

Instead of the asparagus, use 3 small zucchini. Slice them, unpeeled, into lengthwise strips about ¼ inch thick. Toss in a little salt and leave in a colander for 30 minutes, then rinse and dry well. Chargrill them as for the asparagus.

SPANISH OMELET

A flat omelet made with potato and onion is called tortilla española in Spanish. Traditional tortillas use a lot of olive oil, but this recipe proves that this is not really necessary. Serve with a tangy tomato salad.

2 large potatoes, total weight about 1 lb

salt and freshly ground black pepper

1 Spanish onion

6 eggs

2 tablespoons olive oil

1 tablespoon chopped fresh flat-leaf parsley, to serve

Serves 4

Preparation time: 15 minutes
Cooking time: 35–45 minutes

1   Halve or quarter the potatoes, depending on their size, then cook them in salted boiling water for 15–20 minutes, or until just tender.

2   Drain the potatoes, leave until cool enough to handle, then cut into dice. Coarsely chop the onion. Beat the eggs in a bowl with salt and pepper to taste.

3   Heat the oil in a deep, non-stick skillet, add the onion and diced potatoes, and fry over low heat for 10–15 minutes, stirring frequently, until soft and golden. Meanwhile, preheat the broiler.

4   Add the eggs to the skillet and draw the edges of the egg into the center with a fork, letting the runny egg flow to the sides. Cook undisturbed until the eggs are just beginning to set in the center, about 5 minutes. Slide the omelet under the hot broiler and cook for a few minutes until the top is golden brown.

To Serve   Slide the omelet out onto a plate and sprinkle with the parsley. Serve warm or cold, cut into wedges.

Chef's Tips

In Spain the potatoes are usually peeled for tortilla, but you may prefer to retain the maximum amount of vitamins and minerals by leaving the skins on.

◆

Wedges of cold tortilla are excellent for packed lunches and picnics.

CARAMELIZED ONION TARTLETS

These tartlets look spectacular and taste delicious – crisp, light phyllo cases and a gooey melt-in-the-mouth filling. Serve them for a vegetarian main course followed by a large mixed salad, and one or two of your favorite cheeses.

1 lb red and Spanish onions

2 garlic cloves

a few sprigs of fresh thyme

4–5 tablespoons olive oil

8 rectangular sheets of phyllo pastry (see Chef's Tip)

4 small fresh thyme sprigs, to serve

Serves 4

Preparation time: 15–20 minutes
Cooking time: 40–50 minutes

1   Thinly slice the onions. Finely chop the garlic and thyme leaves. Heat 2 tablespoons oil in a non-stick skillet, add the onions, garlic, and thyme, and cook over low heat until caramelized and golden, 35–40 minutes. Stir often during this time, to prevent sticking.

2   Meanwhile, preheat the oven to 375°F, and put a large cookie sheet in the oven to heat at the same time. Brush the insides of four 4–5 inch tart pans lightly with oil.

3   Cut the phyllo into sixteen 7 inch squares. Brush 1 square lightly with oil and place it in one of the pans, tucking the pastry into the inside edge. Brush another square with oil and place it on top of the first, arranging it so that the points are at different angles from the first and tucking it well in at the inside edge. Repeat with a third and fourth square, then prick the base of the phyllo all over with a fork, and fill with crumpled foil. Repeat with the remaining 3 tart pans.

4   Put the tart tins on the hot cookie sheet and bake blind for 5 minutes. Remove the foil, return the tins to the oven, and bake for a further 2 minutes or until the pastry is golden brown. Remove the tartlets from the oven and set them aside to cool a little in the tins.

To Serve   Transfer the filo cases to plates, then spoon in the onion mixture and garnish each tartlet with a sprig of thyme. Serve warm.

Chef's Tip

Phyllo pastry is available frozen in boxes at most supermarkets and Middle Eastern stores. Most boxes contain rectangular sheets in a roll, which must be thawed before they can be unrolled. Sizes vary according to manufacturer, so you may need more or less sheets than the number given here, which is based on the sheets being 12 x 7 inches. Filo pastry is very fragile and it dries out very quickly when it is exposed to air. Always keep the pieces you are not actually working with covered with cling film or a damp cloth.

ASPARAGUS WITH HAZELNUT DRESSING

Fresh young homegrown asparagus appears in the shops in May and June. This simple way of cooking and serving it is one of the best – the flavors in the dressing complement the asparagus perfectly without masking its natural flavor.

1 lb slender asparagus spears

2 tablespoons lemon juice

2 tablespoons finely chopped fresh flat-leaf parsley

2 tablespoons hazelnut oil

freshly ground black pepper

1 teaspoon sea or rock salt

Serves 4

Preparation time: 10 minutes
Cooking time: about 4 minutes

1   Wash the asparagus spears and trim off any thick or woody ends. Pour water into a large sauté pan to come 2–3 inches up the sides. Bring the water to simmering point and add the asparagus. Simmer until just tender, about 4 minutes, depending on the thickness of the stalks.

2   Meanwhile, put the lemon juice in a jug with the parsley, oil, and pepper to taste and whisk together with a fork.

3   Drain the asparagus, spread out on a clean cloth and pat dry.

To Serve   Transfer the asparagus to a serving plate and sprinkle with the sea salt. Whisk the dressing again and spoon it carefully over the asparagus so that each stalk has some dressing on it. Serve warm or at room temperature.

Chef's Tip

The asparagus can be left to soak in the dressing several hours ahead of serving, so it makes an ideal first course for a dinner party. Made in larger quantities, it is also good for a summer buffet or barbecue.

◆

Variations

If you prefer, you can chargrill the asparagus rather than boiling it. Heat a little olive oil on a ridged, cast-iron griddle pan, add the asparagus and cook for 5–8 minutes, turning once.

◆

For a change, use shredded basil instead of parsley.

5

Pulses, grains & pasta

The Mediterranean diet makes full use of pulses, grains, and pasta. These, together with fresh fruit, vegetables, and fish, and a moderate amount of meat, make people in the Mediterranean some of the healthiest in the world. Natural partners in a vegetarian diet, pulses and grains come together to make a protein that is just as good as the protein we get from fish or meat, a nutritional miracle that has long been recognized in the poorer parts of the world.

Necessity is the mother of invention, and there are thousands of wonderful recipes using pasta, pulses, and grains. Without much taste of their own, they readily take on the flavors of other ingredients – as the recipes in this chapter illustrate so well. The pungency of spices, tastiness of garlic and onions, the freshness of herbs, sweetness of fresh and dried fruits, and the heat of chilies: these are just a few examples of the flavors they marry well with.

Fat cannot be completely avoided in light cooking, and for good health it is essential – in moderation. You will notice that many of the recipes specify olive oil. This is the best "fat" to use in light and healthy dishes, because it is a monounsaturated oil, better for the heart than saturated animal fats like butter. Get into the habit of using it whenever you would normally use butter or another fat.

TABBOULEH

This Middle Eastern dish made from bulgar is full of flavor, and a favorite salad with vegetarians. It is usually made with lots of fresh herbs and is very green, but you can use less if you prefer. Serve with warm pita or other Middle Eastern bread.

1¾ cups bulgar wheat

1 x 14 oz can chopped tomatoes

2 cups fresh mint

2 shallots

2 cups fresh flat-leaf parsley

2 cups fresh cilantro

grated rind and juice of 1 lemon

2 tablespoons extra virgin olive oil

Serves 4–6

Preparation time: 20 minutes, plus standing time

1   Rinse the wheat in a sieve under cold running water. Squeeze out the excess water and place the wheat in a bowl.

2   Bring the chopped tomatoes to a boil in a saucepan, pour them over the wheat and stir well with a fork. Leave to stand for 1 hour, stirring occasionally, until the wheat has absorbed the tomato juices and softened.

3   Reserve a few whole mint sprigs for the garnish. Finely chop the remaining mint leaves with the shallots, parsley, and cilantro. Mix into the wheat with the remaining ingredients. Season well and set aside at room temperature for at least 15–20 minutes.

To Serve   Taste for seasoning, turn into a serving bowl and garnish with the reserved whole mint sprigs. Serve at room temperature.

Chef's Tips

Bulgar, also called bulgur and burghul, is boiled and dried wheat. You can buy it in supermarkets, health food shops and Middle Eastern stores. It does not need to be cooked, but it does need soaking so that it becomes soft enough to eat. Hot water is generally used, but this recipe uses hot tomatoes and their juice for flavor and color.

Tightly covered with cling film, tabbouleh will keep in the refrigerator for up to 24 hours, but remember to let it come to room temperature before serving. If it is too cold, it will lack flavor.

FRAGRANT CHICKPEA PILAF

Cinnamon and toasted cumin give this simple pilaf a subtle, spicy fragrance and flavor. It makes a nutritious vegetarian main course served with plain yogurt, or it can be served as a side dish with meat. It goes really well with lamb kebabs.

2 teaspoons cumin seeds

2 onions

2 celery sticks

1 tablespoon olive oil

2 cinnamon sticks

1 cup plus 2 tablespoons white long-grain rice

4 cups hot vegetable stock

1 x 14 oz can chickpeas

salt and freshly ground black pepper

chopped fresh cilantro, to serve

Serves 4–6

Preparation time: 10–15 minutes
Cooking time: 35 minutes

Chef's Tip

This pilaf needs a flavorsome stock. Buy chilled fresh vegetable stock, available at supermarkets.

◆

Variation

Color the rice yellow by sprinkling a pinch of saffron threads into the stock in step 3. Stir well before covering the pan.

1   Dry-fry the cumin seeds in a non-stick skillet over low heat for a few minutes, stirring them constantly until they are lightly browned. Remove them from the skillet and crush with a pestle and mortar. Finely chop the onions and celery.

2   Heat the oil in a large non-stick sauté pan and sauté the onions, celery, cinnamon sticks, and cumin for about 10 minutes, or until the onions are tinged golden brown. Add the rice and stir for 2 minutes.

3   Pour in the hot stock and let it sizzle, then lower the heat, cover the pan, and simmer gently until the rice is al dente, about 20 minutes.

4   Add the chickpeas, season well, and heat through.

To Serve   Turn into a warm serving dish, remove the cinnamon sticks if you like, and sprinkle with chopped cilantro. Serve hot.

MUSHROOM AND PEARL BARLEY RISOTTO

Pearl barley makes a creamy risotto with a nutty bite. It can be served Italian style as a first course for six people, or American style as a vegetarian main course for four, with a tossed green salad and a selection of cheeses to follow.

1 cup plus 2 tablespoons pearl barley

4 cups vegetable stock

2 bay leaves

salt and freshly ground black pepper

2 shallots

2 garlic cloves

2 cups button mushrooms

2 tablespoons butter

2 tablespoons low-fat crème fraîche

4 tablespoons chopped fresh flat-leaf parsley

Serves 4–6

Preparation time: 10–15 minutes
Cooking time: 45 minutes

Chef's Tip

Pearl barley is barley grain that has been hulled and polished – or "pearled." It has a special affinity with mushrooms and lamb, and is often used in soups and stews as a thickener. Look for it in the supermarket or health food shop next to the rice and other grains.

◆

Variation

If you like, top with coarsely grated Italian Parmesan or pecorino cheese, or the hard, salty ricotta salata. You could also use the Spanish manchego.

1   Put the barley in a large saucepan and cover with cold water. Bring to a boil, drain, and rinse under the cold tap. Drain again, then return to the rinsed pan. Add the stock, bay leaves, and salt and pepper to taste. Bring slowly to a boil, then half cover and simmer for 20 minutes.

2   Meanwhile, finely chop the shallots and garlic. Quarter or halve the mushrooms, depending on their size. Melt the butter in a wide, deep sauté pan and stir-fry the shallots for 2 minutes. Add the mushrooms and garlic and stir-fry for 4–5 minutes until tinged brown.

3   Add the mushroom mixture to the pearl barley, season and stir well, then continue to simmer for 20 minutes, or until the barley is al dente. Most of the liquid should be absorbed, but the risotto should have a creamy, soupy consistency.

4   Remove from the heat, cover, and leave to stand for 5 minutes, then remove the bay leaves and gently stir in the crème fraîche and about half the parsley. Taste for seasoning.

To Serve   Divide the risotto between warm soup plates and sprinkle with the remaining parsley. Serve immediately.

GREEN LENTIL SALAD

This is a colorful salad that can be made all year round, but it is especially good for picnics and other al fresco meals, served with cold chicken or cooked meats. It is also good on its own, with wholemeal or granary bread, and with cheese.

1 cup green lentils

salt and freshly ground black pepper

1 red bell pepper

1 orange bell pepper

6 scallions

1 lemon

½ green dessert apple

2 tablespoons hazelnut, walnut, or sesame oil

Serves 4–6

Preparation time: 20 minutes
Cooking time: 35–45 minutes

Chef's Tip

Green lentils hold their shape during cooking and are excellent in salads. Look for them in Middle Eastern stores and health food shops, as well as in supermarkets. If you can get the French Puy lentils, these are considered the finest. They are smaller than other green lentils, and are tinged grey-black.

1   Rinse the lentils in a sieve under cold running water. Place them in a saucepan, cover generously with cold water, and add a pinch of salt. Bring to a boil and remove any scum, then simmer until tender, 30–40 minutes. If necessary, add more water if it becomes absorbed by the lentils during this time.

2   While the lentils are cooking, core, deseed, and dice the peppers. Thinly slice the scallions. Grate the lemon rind and squeeze the juice. Core and dice the apple, place in a large bowl and immediately toss in the lemon juice. Add the lemon rind, bell peppers, and scallions and toss well to mix.

3   Drain the lentils into a sieve and rinse with hot water from the kettle, then mix with the other ingredients while still hot. Add the oil and plenty of salt and pepper and stir well.

To Serve   Taste for seasoning and transfer to a serving bowl. Serve warm or at room temperature.

Red rice salad

Charred corn gives this colorful vegetable and rice salad a smoky flavor, and it goes really well with barbecued chicken or meat. If you like, you can cook the corn on the barbecue too.

¾ cup red rice

salt and freshly ground black pepper

1 corn cob

1 red bell pepper

1–2 red chilies

4 ripe plum tomatoes

6 inch piece of cucumber

4 scallions

2 cups fresh flat-leaf parsley

3 tablespoons extra virgin olive oil

2 tablespoons red wine vinegar

Serves 4

Preparation time: 20 minutes
Cooking time: 45 minutes

Chef's Tips

Red rice comes from the Camargue in southern France. It is quite easy to get in supermarkets and delicatessens, but you can use brown rice instead – they both have a similar nutty flavor.

◆

If you leave the seeds in the chilies, the salad will be spicy hot. When you taste it for seasoning before serving, add a drop or two of Tabasco if you want a hotter flavor.

1 Preheat the broiler to hot. Place the rice in a medium saucepan of salted water and bring to a boil. Simmer gently, uncovered, for about 30 minutes, or until the rice is just tender. Remove from the heat, cover the pan, and leave to stand.

2 Remove the husk and silks from the outside of the corn and place under the hot broiler for about 15 minutes, turning several times until the corn is charred on all sides. Leave until cool enough to handle, then stand the corn upright on a chopping board and cut off the kernels using a downward action with a sharp knife.

3 Turn the rice into a sieve and rinse under the cold tap until cool. Set aside to drain well. Halve, core, and deseed the bell pepper and chilies, then finely dice them. Finely dice the tomatoes, cucumber, and scallions. Finely chop the parsley.

4 Mix the drained rice with the corn and vegetables. Whisk the oil and vinegar together in a jug, pour over the salad and fork through. Add seasoning to taste.

To Serve Turn the salad into a serving bowl and serve at room temperature.

SPICED FRUITY COUSCOUS

Dried fruit and cumin seeds give couscous a sweet and spicy flavor.
Serve as a vegetarian main course with a raita of yogurt, cucumber,
and mint, or as a side dish with broiled or barbecued meat.

2 teaspoons cumin seeds

2¼ cups vegetable stock

1 cup couscous

½ cup ready-to-eat prunes

½ cup ready-to-eat dried apricots

2 tablespoons extra virgin olive oil

2 tablespoons chopped fresh cilantro

salt and freshly ground black pepper

Serves 4–6

Preparation time: 15 minutes
Cooking time: 10 minutes, plus
standing time

Chef's Tip

*The couscous you buy in packets at
supermarkets and health food
shops is precooked, and only needs
soaking in hot liquid or very short
cooking to become light and fluffy.
It is made from steamed and dried
semolina grains, and is part of the
staple diet of North Africa, where it
is most often steamed over meat
and vegetable stews.*

1   Dry-fry the cumin seeds over low heat in a non-stick skillet for a
few minutes, stirring constantly. Crush the seeds finely with a pestle
and mortar and set aside.

2   Bring the stock to a boil in a large saucepan, add the couscous and
stir well. Turn off the heat, cover the pan tightly with the lid, and leave
to stand for 10 minutes.

3   Fork the couscous through. Using scissors, snip the dried fruit into
the couscous, then add the cumin seeds, oil, half the cilantro, and salt
and pepper to taste. Fork through until evenly mixed.

To Serve   Turn the couscous into a serving bowl and sprinkle with
the remaining cilantro. Serve hot or at room temperature.

LEMON, PARSLEY, AND PINE NUT PASTA

Quick and easy, this is one of the new-style pasta dishes. A handful of raw ingredients is simply tosssed with hot pasta and dressing to make a high energy meal that is literally bursting with fresh flavor. Serve it for a first or main course, topped with thin shavings of Parmesan or pecorino if you like.

¾ lb dried pasta twists

salt and freshly ground black pepper

2 cups fresh flat-leaf parsley

1 lemon

6 tablespoons extra virgin olive oil

2 tablespoons balsamic vinegar

½ cup pine nuts, toasted

1   Cook the pasta in salted boiling water for 10 minutes or according to package instructions.

2   Meanwhile, finely chop the parsley, then grate the lemon rind and squeeze the juice. Place in a large bowl with the oil, vinegar, and salt and pepper to taste and stir well to mix.

3   Drain the pasta, add to the dressing with about half the pine nuts and toss well to mix.

To Serve   Taste for seasoning and sprinkle with the remaining pine nuts. Serve immediately.

Serves 4–6

Preparation time: 15 minutes
Cooking time: 10 minutes

Chef's Tips

Balsamic vinegar comes from Modena in northern Italy. Genuine aceto balsamico tradizionale di Modena is controlled by Italian law and is aged in wooden barrels for at least 10–12 years. It has an exquisite aroma and flavor, but it is very expensive. For everyday use, simply buy the best you can afford. Look for Italian brands with aceto balsamico di Modena on the label.

◆

Creamy-colored, waxy-textured pine nuts are frequently used in Italian cooking, especially in Liguria where they are included in the famous pesto sauce. To toast them, dry-fry over low heat in a non-stick skillet for a few minutes, shaking the pan and stirring the nuts constantly to prevent them from burning.

Spiced dhal

Served with rice, lentil dhal makes a most nutritious meal. The combination of pulse and grain makes protein that is just as good as the protein we get from meat or fish. Plain yogurt is the traditional, healthy accompaniment.

1½ cups red lentils

salt and freshly ground black pepper

2 onions

3 garlic cloves

2 tablespoons vegetable oil

1 teaspoon ground coriander

½ teaspoon fennel seeds

2 red chilies

1 tablespoon chopped fresh cilantro

Serves 4–6

Preparation time: 15 minutes
Cooking time: 25–30 minutes

Chef's Tip

The chili and oil topping for this dhal is called tarka in Indian cookery. A tarka is usually made with ghee (clarified butter) and often has onions and aromatic spices as well as chilies.

◆

Variation

Red lentils cook down to a rough purée and are good for making dhal, but you can use brown or green lentils if you prefer. They take 30–40 minutes to cook and hold their shape better than red lentils.

1   Rinse the lentils in a sieve under cold running water. Place them in a saucepan, cover generously with cold water, and add a pinch of salt. Bring to a boil and remove any scum, then simmer until tender, about 20 minutes. If necessary, add more water if it becomes absorbed by the lentils during this time.

2   Meanwhile, finely chop the onions and garlic. Heat half the oil in a non-stick skillet until hot. Add the onions, garlic, ground coriander, and fennel seeds and stir-fry over low to moderate heat until the onions are soft and caramelized, about 10 minutes.

3   Add the onion mixture to the lentils, season generously, and fork through until evenly mixed. Turn off the heat under the pan, cover tightly and leave to stand.

4   Thinly slice the chilies, including the seeds if you like their heat. Heat the remaining oil in the skillet and stir-fry the chilies quickly for 1–2 minutes over high heat.

To Serve   Turn the dhal into a warm serving dish and top with the chilies and oil, and the chopped cilantro. Serve hot.

WILD RICE WITH RASPBERRIES

Wild rice is the seed of a wild aquatic grass, not a rice at all, but it looks like very long grains of rice. It is a dramatic dark brown, almost black, color. Here it is teamed with a sweet raspberry and orange dressing and the result is sensational.

3 strips of pared orange rind

1 teaspoon coarsely crushed black peppercorns

1 bay leaf

salt and freshly ground black pepper

¼ cup wild rice

½ cup long-grain white rice

1 cup raspberries

4 tablespoons extra virgin olive oil

2 tablespoons orange juice

a few orange slices, to serve

Serves 4

Preparation time: 10–15 minutes
Cooking time: 50–55 minutes

Chef's Tip

Wild rice is expensive and it is often cooked with other rice to make it go further. For convenience and economy, you can buy packets of wild rice and long-grain white rice mixed together. For this recipe you will need ¾ cup. Cook for the length of time given on the packet.

1   Place the orange rind in a large pan with the pepper and bay leaf. Add 4 cups cold water and a good pinch of salt to taste, and bring to the boil. Add the wild rice and simmer for 30 minutes. Add the white rice, stir, and simmer for another 15–20 minutes, or until both types of rice are tender.

2   Meanwhile, purée two-thirds of the raspberries in a food processor or blender, then work through a sieve into a large bowl. Discard the raspberry seeds. Add the oil and orange juice to the purée, and whisk to make a dressing.

3   Drain the rice into a large sieve and discard the orange rind and bay leaf. Turn the rice into the bowl of dressing and fork through gently. Taste and add salt and pepper if necessary.

To Serve   Turn into a warm serving bowl and garnish with the orange slices and remaining raspberries. Serve hot.

PASTICCIO WITH ROASTED VEGETABLES

Pasticcio is the Italian word for a pasta pie that is baked in the oven. Italian cooks don't need a recipe, they simply make it with whatever ingredients they have on the day. It makes a substantial supper.

1 red bell pepper
1 yellow bell pepper
1 eggplant
1 large zucchini
2 garlic cloves
1 teaspoon dried mixed herbs
2 tablespoons olive oil
salt and freshly ground black pepper
½ lb short pasta
1 quantity Chunky Tomato Sauce (page 181)
1 scant cup vegetable stock
2 x 5 oz packages half-fat mozzarella
1 small handful of fresh basil leaves, to serve

Serves 4–6

Preparation time: 20 minutes
Cooking time: 45–60 minutes, plus standing time

Chef's Tip

You can use any shape of pasta you like, either fresh or dried, although you will find there is far more choice with dried shapes than fresh. Rigatoni, penne, conchiglie, fusilli, and garganelli are some of the shapes that are available fresh, and they all work well in baked dishes like this one.

1   Preheat the oven to 400°F. Halve, core, and deseed the bell peppers, then cut them into chunks. Top and tail the eggplant and zucchini and cut them into chunks like the peppers. Crush the garlic.

2   Place the vegetables in a large non-stick roasting pan and mix in the garlic, dried herbs, oil, and salt and pepper to taste. Roast in the oven for 30–40 minutes, or until lightly charred, stirring occasionally.

3   Meanwhile, cook the pasta in salted boiling water according to package instructions until al dente. Drain well. In a separate pan, heat the tomato sauce with the stock. Drain and dice the mozzarella.

4   Place the vegetables and pasta in a large baking dish and mix well. Pour the tomato sauce over and mix in, then put the mozzarella cubes on top. Bake for 15–20 minutes or until melted and golden. Leave to stand for 5–10 minutes before serving.

To Serve   Scatter the basil leaves over the top of the pasticcio and serve hot.

FELAFELS

Little patties made of chickpeas, felafels come from the Middle East, where they are traditionally fried in oil and served in pita bread pockets. Here they are baked, then topped with a yogurt dressing. Served with a salad and pita bread, they make a delicious lunch.

2 x 14 oz cans chickpeas

¼ onion

2 garlic cloves

about 1 cup fresh flat-leaf parsley

about 1 cup fresh cilantro

1 teaspoon ground cumin

1 tablespoon lemon juice

salt and freshly ground black pepper

½ beaten egg

1–2 tablespoons olive oil

fresh flat-leaf parsley, cilantro,
    or mint sprigs, to serve

Dressing

1 small handful of fresh mint

1 garlic clove

1 scant cup 0% fat Greek yogurt

Serves 4–6

Preparation time: 20 minutes,
plus chilling time

Cooking time: 20 minutes

Variation

Felafels make good cocktail appetizers. Shape the mixture into 40 small patties and bake for the same length of time as the larger felafels in the main recipe. Before serving, top each one with a small spoonful of yogurt dressing and a tiny mint sprig.

1   Drain and rinse the chickpeas, then work them in a food processor or blender with the remaining ingredients except the egg and oil. Turn the mixture into a bowl and beat in the egg, then cover and chill in the refrigerator for 30–60 minutes, or longer if more convenient. Meanwhile, preheat the oven to 350°F.

2   With wet hands, shape the mixture into 20 equal-sized balls. Place the felafels on an oiled cookie sheet and flatten them slightly, then brush them with more oil. Bake for 20 minutes, turning them over halfway.

3   Meanwhile, make the dressing. Work the mint, garlic, and yogurt in the food processor or blender, turn into a bowl and add salt and pepper to taste.

To Serve   Place the felafels on a serving platter and spoon the dressing over them. Serve hot, garnished with parsley, cilantro, or mint.

TAGLIATELLE WITH FENNEL, BELL PEPPER, AND TOMATO

This pasta dish is full of Mediterranean flavor – from the fennel, bell peppers, and tomatoes. Serve it for a vegetarian main course with warm olive focaccia or ciabatta and a tossed green salad.

2 fennel bulbs

1 red bell pepper

1 small onion

2 garlic cloves

1–2 tablespoons olive oil

1 x 14 oz can chopped tomatoes

salt and freshly ground black pepper

1 lb fresh tagliatelle

grated Parmesan or pecorino cheese, to serve (optional)

Serves 4

Preparation time: 20 minutes
Cooking time: 30 minutes

Variations

Use 2 large red, orange or yellow bell peppers instead of the fennel.

◆

Use another pasta shape instead of the tagliatelle. The sauce is chunky and robust, best suited to a wide ribbon noodle like pappardelle, or short shapes like penne (quills) or penne rigate (ridged quills).

1   Trim and halve the fennel bulbs, then cut the fennel into strips about ¾ inch wide. Halve the bell pepper and remove the core and seeds. Thinly slice the onion. Crush the garlic.

2   Preheat the broiler. Heat the oil in a medium saucepan, add the onion and garlic and fry gently for 5 minutes, or until softened but not colored. Add the tomatoes and season generously with salt and pepper, then cover and simmer gently for 20 minutes.

3   Meanwhile, put the bell pepper in the broiler pan and place under the broiler for 5–8 minutes until the skin is charred and blistered. Remove and place in a plastic bag to cool slightly. Broil the strips of fennel for 5 minutes or until they are golden brown.

4   Peel off the pepper skin and slice the flesh into strips. Add to the tomato sauce with the fennel.

5   Cook the tagliatelle in salted boiling water for 2–3 minutes or according to package instructions. Drain well and tip into a warm large bowl. Add the tomato sauce and toss to coat.

To Serve   Divide the pasta and sauce between warm soup bowls and serve immediately, with grated cheese if you like.

SMOKY ZUCCHINI AND PECORINO PASTA

The strong, summery flavors of chargrilled zucchini and basil go well with salty pecorino and tangy lime. Serve for a quick, midweek supper with chunky Italian bread like focaccia or ciabatta.

2 small zucchini

3 oz pecorino cheese

4 tablespoons extra virgin olive oil, or more to taste

juice of 1 lime

salt and freshly ground black pepper

¾ lb fresh or dried pappardelle

3 tablespoons fresh basil leaves

Serves 4

Preparation time: 15 minutes
Cooking time: 15–20 minutes

Chef's Tips

Pecorino is a hard Italian cheese similar to Parmesan, but with a slightly sharper, saltier flavor. It is made from sheep's milk.

◆

Pappardelle is a wide, flat ribbon pasta which originated in Tuscany. Traditional pappardelle have wavy edges, but nowadays they are often made with straight edges. You can get them fresh and dried, and they are usually made with egg.

◆

Variation

If you prefer, use lemon instead of lime. It tastes slightly less sharp.

1   Heat a ridged, cast-iron grill pan until very hot. Meanwhile, top and tail the zucchini, then slice them along their length into thin strips. Shave the cheese into ribbons with a potato peeler.

2   Brush about 1 tablespoon olive oil over the zucchini strips, then place them on the pan in batches and chargrill for 1–2 minutes each batch. Turn them with tongs until they are tender and lightly charred on all sides, then transfer them to a bowl.

3   Mix another tablespoon of oil with the lime juice and plenty of seasoning. Drizzle over the zucchini, cover, and set aside.

4   Cook the pasta in salted boiling water according to package instructions until al dente. Drain and turn into a warm large serving bowl. Add the zucchini ribbons and marinade and three-quarters of the basil leaves. Toss gently to mix, then add more oil and seasoning according to taste.

To Serve   Top with the pecorino cheese and the remaining basil leaves and serve immediately.

MUSHROOM RISOTTO CAKES

These make a very tasty vegetarian lunch served with a salad. Made into balls half the size, they are also good for a first course served with a salsa or dip. Tiny balls can be served on cocktail sticks with drinks.

1 cup button or chestnut
   mushrooms
1 cup sliced leek
1 garlic clove
10–12 fresh thyme sprigs
2 tablespoons olive oil
¾ cup risotto rice

2½ cups hot vegetable stock
salt and freshly ground black pepper
1 egg, beaten
about 2 cups fresh wholemeal
   breadcrumbs
lemon wedges and fresh thyme sprigs,
   to serve

Serves 4

Preparation time: 15 minutes,
plus cooling time
Cooking time: 50 minutes

1   Finely chop the mushrooms, leek, and garlic. Strip the leaves from the sprigs of thyme and chop them finely.

2   Heat the oil in a non-stick skillet and gently fry the chopped mushrooms, leek, and garlic until soft. Add the rice and stir over low to moderate heat for 1–2 minutes, then pour in about one-third of the stock and stir well. Season to taste, then simmer uncovered until the stock is absorbed, stirring frequently. Add the remaining stock in two stages and continue to simmer and stir until all the liquid has been absorbed and the rice is tender and quite dry, 15–20 minutes.

3   Remove the pan from the heat and stir in the thyme. Taste for seasoning. Turn the risotto out on to a large plate or tray and spread it out flat. Leave to cool slightly, 20–30 minutes. Meanwhile, preheat the oven to 350°F.

4   With wet hands, divide the risotto into 8–12 equal-sized balls, squeezing them so that the rice compresses together. Flatten each one slightly, then dip into the beaten egg and then the breadcrumbs.

5   Put the risotto cakes on an oiled cookie sheet and bake in the oven for 20 minutes, or until crisp and golden in color.

To Serve   Transfer the risotto cakes to individual plates, garnish with lemon and thyme, and serve warm.

Chef's Tips

Risotto rice has short, round grains which absorb liquid slowly to become plump and soft with a nutty bite. You will find it at the supermarket labelled as risotto, arborio or carnaroli rice. At Italian delicatessens you may get even more of a choice.

◆

Chop the vegetables and thyme in a food processor. Not only to save time, but to get the very fine texture that is best for these cakes.

◆

These are best served warm. They can be prepared ahead up to the end of step 4.

SMOKED SALMON AND ASPARAGUS LINGUINE

A lemony light hollandaise sauce is used to coat thin strands of
linguine pasta. Combined with smoked salmon and fresh asparagus,
it makes the perfect dish for a spring lunch or supper.

5 oz fine asparagus

6 oz smoked salmon trimmings

salt and freshly ground black pepper

2 eggs

juice of ½ lemon

2 tablespoons chopped fresh dill

10 oz fresh linguine

Serves 3–4

Preparation time: 15–20 minutes
Cooking time: 15 minutes

1   Trim any tough ends off the asparagus, then cut the asparagus
into 2 inch lengths. Cut the salmon into thin strips.

2   Cook the asparagus in salted boiling water until just tender to the
tip of a knife. This will take 2–5 minutes, depending on thickness.
Remove the asparagus with a slotted spoon and drain on paper towels.
Keep the water hot in the pan.

3   Place the eggs and lemon juice in a round-bottomed bowl. Set the
bowl over a pan of hot water, making sure the bottom of the bowl
does not touch the water. Whisk the eggs until warmed, pale, and very
frothy. Season, and stir in half the dill, then remove the bowl from the
pan and set aside in a warm place.

4   Top up the asparagus water with boiling water and bring back to a
boil, then add the linguine. Boil for 2–3 minutes, or according to
package instructions, until al dente.

5   Drain the linguine, reserving the water, then return the linguine to
the pan. Add the asparagus and salmon with 1 ladleful of the water
and the lemon sauce. Toss and add more water if necessary.

To Serve   Transfer the linguine to warm bowls and sprinkle with the
remaining dill. Serve immediately.

Chef's Tips

*Smoked salmon trimmings,
sometimes called "cocktail salmon,"
are much cheaper than thinly sliced
salmon, yet they are perfectly good
enough for cooking. You can buy
them in packages at supermarkets,
delicatessens and fish markets.*

◆

*Take care not to let the hollandaise
get too hot or the eggs may
scramble or curdle. They need to be
just warm enough to thicken.
Vigorous whisking is essential.*

◆

Variation

*For a special treat, whisk 1–2
tablespoons crème fraîche or
whipping cream into the hollandaise
after removing it from the heat.*

PENNE WITH HONEY ROAST SQUASH

The bright orange, sweet flesh of butternut squash looks and tastes so good when roasted with honey, orange juice, and mustard – and it mingles well with pasta and mature manchego cheese. Serve for a vegetarian main course.

1 butternut squash, weighing about 1¼ lb	1 tablespoon coarsegrain mustard
2 small zucchini	2 tablespoons orange juice
leaves of 1 fresh rosemary sprig	2 oz manchego cheese
salt and freshly ground black pepper	¾ lb fresh penne
1 tablespoon clear honey	⅓ cup hot vegetable stock
	1 tablespoon extra virgin olive oil

Serves 4

Preparation time: 20 minutes
Cooking time: 40–50 minutes

1   Preheat the oven to 400°F. Cut the butternut squash into ¾ inch chunks and remove the peel, seeds, and fibers. Cut the zucchini into similar-size pieces. Place the vegetables in a large non-stick roasting pan. Scatter the rosemary leaves over the vegetables, then sprinkle with a little salt.

2   Mix the honey, mustard, and orange juice in a small bowl. Pour over the vegetables and bake in the oven until the vegetables are tender in the center and crisp around the edges, 40–50 minutes. Turn them gently once or twice during roasting so they color evenly.

3   Meanwhile, thinly slice the cheese with a vegetable peeler. Cook the pasta in salted boiling water according to package instructions until al dente.

4   Turn the roasted vegetables into a warm bowl and deglaze the roasting pan with the stock.

5   Drain the pasta and add to the vegetables with the deglazed pan juices. Toss well to mix, then taste for seasoning.

To Serve   Transfer to warm bowls and sprinkle the oil and cheese over the top. Serve immediately.

Chef's Tips

Butternut squash is a pear-shaped squash with hard green skin and bright orange flesh. It is a winter vegetable, although it can be found at other times of the year. Pumpkin can be used instead.

Manchego is a creamy yellow sheep's milk cheese from Spain with a mild, buttery flavor. You can buy it young and fresh, but for this recipe a mature, ripe manchego is most suitable. You could use Gruyère or Emmental instead, both of which also melt well over hot pasta.

FRESH HERB RISOTTO

This is a versatile risotto, delicious in spring or summer when soft and leafy fresh herbs have their best flavor, but it can also be made in winter with a change of herbs. Serve it as a first course for 6 people, or as a main course for four, with bread and a salad.

1 onion
2 garlic cloves
1 tablespoon olive oil
1 cup and 2 tablespoons risotto rice
½ cup dry white wine
3½ cups hot vegetable stock
salt and freshly ground black pepper
3 tablespoons chopped mixed fresh herbs
grated rind of 1 lemon

Serves 4–6

Preparation time: 10 minutes
Cooking time: 25–30 minutes

Chef's Tip

Summer herbs, such as basil, oregano, marjoram, and parsley, are all good choices and you can use just one or two of them or a mixture. In the winter, you could use parsley, sage, or thyme, but take care not to use too much sage because it has a strong flavor.

1   Finely chop the onion and garlic. Heat the oil in a medium saucepan and gently cook the onion and garlic until soft. Add the rice and stir over low to moderate heat for 1–2 minutes, then pour in the wine and let it sizzle.

2   Pour in one-third of the stock and stir well. Season to taste, then simmer until the stock is absorbed, stirring frequently. Add the remaining stock in two stages and continue to simmer and stir until all the liquid has been absorbed and the rice is tender, 15–20 minutes.

3   Remove from the heat and stir in 2 tablespoons of the fresh herbs and the lemon rind. Season well.

To Serve   Divide the risotto equally between warm soup bowls and sprinkle with the remaining herbs. Serve immediately.

SUMMER PEA AND SAGE RISOTTO

Risottos make ideal summer food because they are quick to make. Freshly shelled peas are sweet at the beginning of the season, so make this risotto in early summer as soon as you see them in the shops.

1 lb young fresh peas, unshelled
    weight
3 fresh sage sprigs
6 white peppercorns
salt and freshly ground black pepper
1 white onion

1 teaspoon pink peppercorns
2 tablespoons olive oil
10 oz risotto rice
⅓ cup dry white wine
4 tablespoons low-fat crème fraîche
    or sour cream, to serve

Serves 4

Preparation time: 10 minutes
Cooking time: 30 minutes

Variation

To make a more substantial main course meal for 4 people, top each serving with a poached egg. Bring a wide sauté pan of water to a boil and stir in 1 tablespoon white wine vinegar. Gently break 4 eggs into the water. Remove from the heat, cover, and leave to stand for 3–4 minutes until the eggs are softly poached.

1   Shell the peas. Wash the pea pods and place them in a large saucepan. Add 6¼ cups cold water, 2 whole sage sprigs, the white peppercorns, and a pinch of salt. Bring to a boil and simmer for 5 minutes, then strain the stock into another saucepan. Discard the pea pods and flavorings and keep the stock hot.

2   Finely chop the onion. Crush the pink peppercorns. Strip the leaves off the remaining sage sprig and set aside some small whole leaves for the garnish. Finely chop the rest.

3   Heat the oil in a heavy saucepan and sweat the onion over low heat for about 5 minutes without coloring. Add the rice and stir for about 2 minutes. Add the wine and simmer until evaporated. Stir in the peppercorns, chopped sage, and salt and pepper to taste.

4   Begin to add the hot stock to the rice a ladleful at a time, stirring between each addition until the rice has absorbed the liquid. Add the peas after about 10 minutes, then continue adding stock and stirring for another 10 minutes, or until the rice is al dente and the consistency of the risotto is creamy. You may not need all of the liquid.

To Serve   Taste the risotto for seasoning, then divide between warm soup bowls. Top each serving with a spoonful of crème fraîche and a few sage leaves. Serve immediately.

WILD RICE AND TOMATO SALAD

The contrasting colors of the black, red, and green ingredients in this simple salad make it look dramatic. Serve it as a side dish to hot chargrilled or barbecued meat – it goes well with chicken or steak.

½ cup wild rice

salt and freshly ground black pepper

6–8 sun-dried tomatoes

4 oz cherry tomatoes

about 6 cups lamb's lettuce, to serve

Dressing

2 teaspoons honey

2 tablespoons balsamic vinegar

1 tablespoon walnut oil

1 tablespoon olive oil

Serves 4

Preparation time: 15 minutes
Cooking time: 45–50 minutes

Chef's Tips

Wild rice is not a rice at all, but an aquatic grass which looks like brown-black grains of rice. It can be used instead of rice whenever you want a change of color, but it takes longer to cook – and it costs more. Its nutty flavor and striking good looks make it well worth the extra expense.

◆

Lamb's lettuce is also called mâche. It has pretty little leaves and a delicate flavor, and is often sold in small bunches. Some supermarkets sell it ready trimmed and washed in small plastic boxes or packets.

1   Cook the wild rice in plenty of salted boiling water for about 45–50 minutes, or until tender. Drain into a sieve and rinse under the cold tap until the rice is cold. Allow to drain thoroughly.

2   Slice the sun-dried tomatoes and halve the cherry tomatoes. Put them in a large bowl, add the wild rice, and toss to mix.

3   Make the dressing. In a small bowl, mix together the honey, vinegar, and oils with salt and pepper to taste.

To Serve   Line a shallow serving dish with the lamb's lettuce, pile the rice and tomato salad in the center and drizzle the dressing over. Serve at room temperature.

CHICKPEA, RED ONION, AND CILANTRO SALAD

Chickpeas are a favorite with vegetarians because they have a crunchy bite and a nutty flavor that goes well with so many different ingredients. This simple salad is bursting with zingy flavors. Serve it with warm wholemeal pita bread.

1 cup plus 2 tablespoons chickpeas, soaked in cold water overnight

4 tablespoons extra virgin olive oil

juice of 1 lemon

salt and freshly ground black pepper

1 red onion

1 bunch of fresh cilantro

2 garlic cloves

Serves 4

Preparation time: 20 minutes, plus soaking time

Cooking time: about 2 hours

1 Drain and rinse the chickpeas, place them in a saucepan of fresh cold water and bring to a boil. Skim off any scum, then half cover and simmer for 1½–2 hours or until tender, stirring and topping up the water level as needed.

2 Drain the chickpeas and place them in a large bowl. Add the oil, lemon juice, and salt and pepper to taste, and toss well.

3 Cut a few thin rings from the onion and set aside. Roughly chop the rest. Roughly chop the cilantro and garlic. Add the chopped onion, garlic, and cilantro to the chickpeas, toss to mix thoroughly, then taste for seasoning.

To Serve Turn the salad into a large serving bowl and garnish with the reserved red onion rings. Serve as soon as possible.

Chef's Tip

Serve with wedges of your favorite cheese for a vegetarian main course, or with canned tuna for non-vegetarians.

◆

Variation

Use two 14 oz cans chickpeas instead of dried peas. Drain and rinse them well, then heat them through in the olive oil, lemon juice, and seasoning before adding the remaining ingredients.

LIMA BEANS WITH BROCCOLI AND TOMATO

Sweet juicy plum tomatoes are roasted with garlic and fresh herbs, then tossed with creamy lima beans and tender-crisp broccoli florets to make a tasty vegetarian main course. Serve with nutty brown rice for a nutritious meal.

½ cup olive oil

2 cups dried lima beans, soaked in cold water overnight

1 lb ripe plum tomatoes

2 garlic cloves

1 tablespoon fresh thyme leaves

2 teaspoons fresh marjoram leaves

salt and freshly ground black pepper

juice of ½ lemon

8–10 oz broccoli florets

Serves 6

Preparation time: 20 minutes, plus soaking time

Cooking time: about 1½ hours

1 Preheat the oven to 350°F. Brush a non-stick roasting pan lightly with oil. Drain and rinse the beans, place them in a saucepan of fresh cold water and bring to a boil. Skim off any scum, then half cover and simmer for 1¼ hours or until tender, stirring and topping up the water level as needed.

2 While the beans are cooking, halve the tomatoes lengthwise and scoop out the seeds. Place them cut-side uppermost in the roasting pan. Roughly chop the garlic and herbs and sprinkle them evenly over the tomatoes, with salt and pepper to taste. Drizzle with half the remaining oil, then roast for 1 hour.

3 Drain the beans and place them in a large bowl with the lemon juice, the remaining oil, and plenty of salt and pepper. Turn the beans in the dressing until evenly coated. Add the tomatoes and toss to mix thoroughly.

4 Plunge the broccoli florets into a saucepan of salted boiling water and boil for 3 minutes, until cooked but still quite crisp. Drain thoroughly and pat dry with paper towels or a cloth, then add to the beans and tomatoes and toss gently to mix.

To Serve Taste for seasoning, then transfer to a warm serving dish. Serve warm.

Variations

Use two 14 oz cans lima beans instead of dried beans. Drain and rinse them well, then heat them through in the lemon juice and olive oil before tossing them with the roasted tomatoes.

As an alternative to lima beans, dried white beans can be used, or two 14 oz cans cannellini beans.

Vegetable paella

Fennel, shallots, and tomatoes replace the usual chicken and shellfish in this vegetarian version of paella, which is subtly spiced with cilantro. Serve it as a main course for lunch or dinner, with crusty farmhouse bread and a leafy green side salad.

3 tablespoons olive oil

2 small fennel bulbs

7–8 oz cherry tomatoes

2 teaspoons coriander seeds

salt and freshly ground black pepper

3½ cups hot vegetable stock

½ cup wild rice

1 cup long-grain white rice

2 tablespoons chopped fresh cilantro

juice of ½–1 lemon, to taste

Serves 4

Preparation time: 15 minutes
Cooking time: 50–55 minutes

Variation

Use all white rice instead of the mixture of wild and white rice, and color it yellow by adding a good pinch of saffron threads to the water at the beginning of boiling.

1   Preheat the oven to 400°F. Brush a non-stick roasting pan lightly with oil. Cut each fennel bulb lengthwise into eighths, leaving a little trimmed stalk attached to the base of each section to hold it together. Peel the shallots and halve them lengthwise, or quarter them if they are large. Halve the tomatoes. Lightly crush the coriander seeds.

2   Place the vegetables in the roasting pan and sprinkle the coriander seeds and salt and pepper to taste over them. Roast the vegetables, turning them once or twice, for about 40 minutes, or until tender.

3   Meanwhile, bring the stock to a boil in a large saucepan. Add the wild rice and simmer for 30 minutes, then add the white rice and continue to cook for 15–20 minutes, or until both types of rice are tender. Drain, retaining a little moisture.

To Serve   Turn the rice and roasted vegetables into a large bowl and toss to mix. Add the chopped cilantro and the juice of ½ lemon, then taste for seasoning and add more lemon juice if you like. Serve hot.

6

DESSERTS

Fresh fruit is hard to beat at the end of a meal, especially in the summer when there is such a wide choice of sweet and luscious fruits in season. A platter of plump, ripe fruits looks sensational, and if they are locally grown and ripe they will have the flavor to match. Nutritionists recommend we eat five pieces of fruit and vegetables per day, so if you can get into the habit of drawing meals to a close with fresh fruit you are well on the way to healthy eating.

Fruit provides us with vitamins, minerals, and fiber, plus energy from the natural sugars it contains. We also get sweet and tangy flavors that are immensely refreshing at the end of a meal. The recipes in this chapter concentrate on fruit because it is light and low in fat, but there are many other ingredients you can enjoy when you are cooking light. Yogurt, fromage frais, and crème fraîche combine beautifully with fruit to make creamy desserts that seem anything but low-fat. Sweet wines and liqueurs accentuate fruitiness. Spices offer exotic and unusual flavors.

Dessert is the grand finale of a meal and presentation is very important. Dainty sprigs of mint, edible flowers, and tiny clusters of fruit look just as tempting on top of a dinner party dessert as scrolls of chocolate or swirls of cream. And the good thing is – they are much better for you.

LIME CHEESES WITH GREEN FRUIT SALAD

The beauty of this dessert is that it looks and tastes cool and refreshing. The lime cheeses are exquisitely light, and the fruit salad a striking contrast. Serve for a dinner party in summer when galia melons are sweet and ripe.

1 cup fromage frais
grated rind and juice of 2 limes
1 scant cup whipping cream
¼–⅓ cup confectioner's sugar, to taste
4 fresh mint sprigs, to serve

Fruit Salad
3 ripe kiwi fruit
1 small ripe galia melon

Serves 4

Preparation time: 20–30 minutes, plus chilling time

Variations

If galia melon is difficult to get, use another green-fleshed melon such as an ogen.

◆

In winter, use seedless green grapes or green-skinned apples instead of the melon.

1   Line four ⅔ cup custard dishes with cling film or dampened muslin, letting it hang over the edges.

2   Put the fromage frais and lime rind and juice in a bowl and beat well until smooth. Whip the cream until it just holds its shape and fold it into the cheese. Sift in confectioner's sugar to taste.

3   Spoon the mixture into the dishes, cover with the overhanging cling film or muslin, and chill for up to 8 hours, preferably overnight.

4   A few hours before serving, prepare the fruit over a bowl to catch the juice. Peel the kiwi fruit and slice them into rounds or wedges. Halve the melon and scoop out the seeds, then scoop the flesh into balls with a melon baller or cut it into small chunks with a knife. Gently combine the fruit in a bowl with the juice, then cover and chill until serving time.

To Serve   Unfold the cling film or muslin and place an inverted chilled plate on top of each dish. Turn the cheeses out on to the plates and remove the cling film. Spoon the fruit around, then top each serving with a sprig of mint. Serve chilled.

WILD STRAWBERRY CREAMS

Wild strawberries go by the pretty French name of fraises des bois. They are tiny with an intense flavor, but they are only in season for a very short time in the summer. If you can't get them, use very small strawberries and slice them, or use raspberries.

4 tablespoons grenadine

4 eggs

¼ cup caster sugar

½ teaspoon vanilla extract

1¾ cups milk

3 oz fraises des bois

To Serve

about 7 oz fraises des bois

4 tablespoons grenadine

2 tablespoons caster sugar, or to taste

Serves 4

Preparation time: 20–30 minutes, plus cooling and chilling time
Cooking time: 30–40 minutes

1   Preheat the oven to 300°F. Pour 1 tablespoon grenadine into each of four 1 cup molds.

2   Beat the eggs and sugar in a bowl with the vanilla extract. Scald the milk in a saucepan and slowly stir it into the egg mixture. Strain into a jug, then pour into the molds. The grenadine will mix into the milk, but then sink back to the bottom. Hull the fraises des bois and divide them between the molds. They will float.

3   Place the molds gently in a bain marie of hot water and bake in the oven until just set, about 30–40 minutes. Leave to cool, then cover and chill in the refrigerator for at least 4 hours.

4   A few hours before serving, set aside 4 of the prettiest fraises des bois for the decoration. Hull the rest and place them in a bowl. Sprinkle with the grenadine and sugar to taste, cover, and chill in the refrigerator until serving time.

To Serve   Loosen the top of each set cream with your fingers or by running a knife around the edge. Invert a chilled plate over each mold, then turn the cream out on to the plate. Spoon the fraises des bois and juices over and around the creams and decorate the tops with reserved unhulled fraises des bois. Serve chilled.

Chef's Tips

Grenadine is a scarlet-red fruit syrup. It takes its name from the island of Grenada in the Caribbean, where it was originally made from pomegranate juice, but nowadays it is also made with other fruit juices. Check the label because sometimes it is alcoholic and sometimes not. You can use either. It is generally available at wine merchants and supermarkets, but if you can't get it you can use blackcurrant syrup or the blackcurrant liqueur, crème de cassis, instead.

◆

Dariole molds are the best molds to use because they have rounded bottoms, but soufflé dishes can also be used.

WARM SPICED PEARS

This is a classic winter dessert that never fails to please. It is simple, but it tastes superb. If you like, sprinkle the pears with a few toasted flaked almonds for a crunchy contrast in textures, and serve with chilled low-fat crème fraîche or plain yogurt.

1 packed cup granulated sugar

1 cup red wine

1 cinnamon stick

5 cloves

pared rind of 1 orange

pared rind of 1 lemon

8 pears

juice of ½ lemon

Serves 4

Preparation time: 20–30 minutes
Cooking time: 50–55 minutes

Chef's Tips

One of the best varieties of pears for poaching is Conference. They are fairly small, with firm flesh that holds its shape well.

If you like, serve the pears in bowls with wide rims and sift cocoa powder lightly over the edges.

1   Put the sugar in a saucepan and add 1 cup of cold water. Heat gently until the sugar has dissolved, then increase the heat and boil for 1 minute. Add the wine, spices, and citrus rinds and simmer for about 10 minutes.

2   Peel the pears. With a small, pointed vegetable peeler, remove the cores from the bottoms of the pears, leaving the stalks intact at the top. Immediately brush the pears with lemon juice, then lower them into the wine mixture. Cover with a circle of waxed paper and cook gently until tender, about 30–35 minutes. Remove from the heat and leave to cool until lukewarm.

3   Lift the pears carefully out of the spiced wine and place in serving bowls. Strain the cooking liquid into a clean pan and boil rapidly until reduced by about half.

To Serve   Pour the spiced wine sauce over and around the pears and serve warm or cold.

ICED MINTED BLACKBERRY SOUFFLÉS

The flavors of mint and blackberries go so well together in these tangy, creamy soufflés. They taste rich and delicious – like iced fruit mousses. Make them in high summer, when fresh blackberries are in season, and serve with crisp, sweet biscuits.

2½ cups blackberries

¼ cup granulated sugar

4 egg whites

¾ cup caster sugar

scant cup whipping cream

1 scant cup plain or Greek yogurt

3 tablespoons crème de menthe

edible flowers and leaves, to decorate (optional)

Serves 8

Preparation time: 20–30 minutes, plus freezing time

Chef's Tip

Crème de menthe is a sweet, mint-flavored liqueur, which may be green or white. You can use either, although the white crème de menthe is best because it will not alter the color of the mixture.

1 Tie waxed paper collars around eight ½ cup glass dishes or soufflé dishes to come about 1 inch above the rims.

2 Dissolve the granulated sugar in a saucepan in ⅓ cup of water. Add the blackberries and simmer for 3–4 minutes, then pour into a food processor or blender. Work to a purée, then pour through a sieve into a bowl to remove the seeds.

3 Whisk the egg whites until stiff, then whisk in the caster sugar a little at a time to make a shiny meringue. Half whip the cream in a separate large bowl, then fold together with the blackberry purée, yogurt, and liqueur. Fold in the meringue.

4 Pour into the prepared dishes, level the surface, and freeze until firm, at least 4 hours.

To Serve Untie and remove the paper collars, then decorate the tops of the soufflés with edible flowers and leaves if you like. Serve immediately.

PEACH AND APRICOT TERRINE WITH MUSCAT

Fruit jelly made with muscat wine is an excellent way to suspend pieces of fruit in a terrine. The flavor is pleasantly sweet and musky. Almonds provide a little crunch, which contrasts with the softness of the jelly, but they can be omitted if you prefer.

1 x 14 oz can peaches in natural juice
1 x 14 oz can apricots in natural juice
½ cup whole blanched almonds
½ vanilla pod, split lengthways
1 cup sweet muscat wine
1 envelope gelatine powder
nasturtium flowers, to decorate

Serves 6

Preparation time: 30 minutes, plus cooling and chilling time

Chef's Tip

Muscat wine is a sweet dessert wine made from muscat grapes. Its color varies but it is usually golden yellow or amber. Muscat de Beaumes-de-Venise and Rivesaltes are two well known muscat wines that are suitable for this recipe.

◆

Variation

Canned pears in natural juice can be used instead of either the peaches or apricots.

1   Drain the peaches and apricots into a sieve over a bowl to catch the juice. Cut the fruit into slices, not too small. Coarsely chop the almonds. Arrange half the fruit in a 2 lb non-stick bread pan. Place the almonds on top and then the remaining fruit.

2   Pour the wine and ⅔ cup of the reserved fruit juice into a saucepan and add the vanilla pod. Bring to a boil and simmer for about 5 minutes, then remove from the heat and leave to cool a little.

3   Sprinkle the gelatine powder over ½ cup of cold water in a small heatproof bowl. Leave for 5 minutes until spongy, then place the bowl in a saucepan of gently simmering water for a few minutes until the gelatine has dissolved.

4   Remove the vanilla pod from the cool wine, then pour in the dissolved gelatine. Stir to mix. Leave until just cold, then slowly pour it over the fruit. Cover and chill in the refrigerator overnight.

To Serve   Invert a chilled plate over the bread pan, then warm the pan by covering it with a hot damp cloth. This will help release the jelly. Turn the jelly out on to the plate and slice with a hot knife. Arrange slices on dessert plates, decorate with nasturtium flowers and serve chilled.

LEMON AND YOGURT ICE

This refreshing, tangy iced dessert is simplicity itself to make. It is good served plain, with dainty sweet biscuits, or you can top it with thinly sliced stem ginger or toasted shredded coconut.

scant cup whipping cream

2¼ cups low-fat plain yogurt

½ cup lemon curd

Serves 4

Preparation time: 10 minutes, plus freezing time

1   In a large bowl, half whip the cream until it just holds its shape. Add the yogurt and fold the two together until smooth. Streak through the lemon curd.

2   Pour the mixture into a freezer container, cover, and freeze until firm, at least 4 hours.

To Serve   Transfer the freezer container to the refrigerator for 10–15 minutes, then scoop into stemmed glasses. Serve immediately.

Chef's Tips

Greek yogurt is smooth and creamy, and there are many different types. One variety is 0% fat. Another good yogurt to use is live culture yogurt.

◆

Use a good-quality, tangy lemon curd. Homemade is best.

Hot rum and citrus salad

The Caribbean meets the Far East in this spiced fruit salad, which combines citrus fruit with exotic mangoes and is subtly flavored with star anise. Served warm with crisp, thin wafers, it is a very useful all-year-round recipe.

5 oranges

3 ruby or pink grapefruit

1 lemon

2 mangoes, slightly under ripe

½ cup soft brown sugar

⅓ cup orange juice

4 tablespoons dark rum

4 star anise, plus extra to serve if liked

Serves 6–8

Preparation time: 20–30 minutes, plus infusing time

Chef's Tip

To segment citrus fruit neatly, cut a thick slice off the top and bottom of the fruit, then cut off the peel all around so that no white pith remains on the fruit. With a small sharp knife, cut vertically between the flesh and the membranes, working all around the fruit until every segment has been released, and you are left with just the core and membranes joined together.

1 Peel and segment the oranges, grapefruit, and lemon. Peel and pit the mangoes, then cut the flesh into pieces of a similar size to the citrus fruit. Put all the fruit in a heatproof serving bowl.

2 Put the sugar in a saucepan, add ⅓ cup cold water, and heat gently until the sugar has dissolved. Add the orange juice, rum, and star anise. Simmer for 10 minutes, then remove from the heat, cover, and leave to infuse for 30 minutes.

To Serve Pour the syrup over the fruit. Decorate the top with star anise if you like (you can use the ones from the syrup) and serve warm.

BAKED APPLES AND FIGS

This is a versatile dessert, which can be made in summer or winter. Apples are in season all year round, fresh figs in the summer, so you can make it with both fruits when they are available – or with just one or the other.

4 small dessert apples

4 large fresh figs, not over ripe

1 tablespoon whole blanched almonds

1 small piece of stem ginger

2 oz marzipan

1 tablespoon syrup from ginger jar

Amaretti Cream

10 amaretti biscuits

1 cup low-fat fromage frais

1 tablespoon sifted confectioner's sugar

1 tablespoon amaretto liqueur (optional)

Serves 4

Preparation time: 20–30 minutes

Cooking time: about 45 minutes

Chef's Tips

Stem ginger is sold in small bottles in the baking sections of supermarkets and in delicatessens. It is sometimes labeled as "preserved ginger in syrup."

1   Preheat the oven to 350°F. Core the apples and score horizontally around their middles with the point of a sharp knife. Cut the figs lengthwise almost through into quarters, leaving them intact at the base.

2   Finely chop the almonds. Very finely chop the ginger. Mix the marzipan, almonds, ginger, and syrup until smooth and roll into 8 cylinders or balls. Place a ball in the center of each fruit.

3   Place the apples in a baking dish with 3 tablespoons cold water and bake for 30 minutes. Add the figs to the dish and bake for another 10–15 minutes, or until both types of fruit are tender.

4   Meanwhile, roughly crush the amaretti biscuits and mix with the remaining ingredients for the amaretti cream.

To Serve   Put 1 apple and 1 fig on each plate and top with a little of the cream. Serve hot, with the remaining cream handed separately.

BLACK CHERRY CRÊPES

Don't deny yourself treats like crêpes when you're eating light. If you make them with low-fat milk and use a fruity, low-fat filling, they are healthy and light. This recipe makes 8 filled crêpes, which can serve 4–8 people.

¾ lb black cherries

1–2 tablespoons confectioner's sugar, to taste

½ cup plus 2 tablespoons low-fat plain yogurt or 0% fat Greek yogurt

2 teaspoons vegetable oil

Crêpe Batter

1 cup all-purpose flour

1 egg

about 1¼ cups low-fat milk

Makes 8

Preparation time: 20 minutes, plus standing time

Cooking time: 20–35 minutes

Chef's Tip

For a lump-free crêpe batter, use an electric mixer for whisking.

◆

Variation

Fresh cherries have a very short season. When they are not available, use bottled cherries, preferably ones that have been macerated in kirsch.

1 First make the crêpe batter. Whisk together the flour, egg, and 1¼ cups milk until smooth. Cover and set aside for 30 minutes.

2 Meanwhile, prepare the filling. Pit the cherries and halve or quarter them if they are large. Stir sugar to taste into the yogurt.

3 Brush a 7 inch non-stick crêpe pan very lightly with oil and heat until hot. Whisk the batter well, and thin it with a little milk if it is too thick. Pour one-eighth of the batter into the hot pan and swirl it around to cover the base. Cook for 1–2 minutes until golden underneath, then turn over and cook the other side. Turn the crêpe out of the pan, first side facing down, and keep warm. Repeat with the remaining mixture to make 8 crêpes altogether, adding more oil as necessary and stacking the crêpes on top of each other as they are done.

To Serve Place a spoonful of sweetened yogurt in the center of each crêpe and top with a spoonful of cherries. Fold the crêpes into quarters and dust with a little sugar. Serve warm.

EXOTIC FRUIT PAVLOVAS

Pavlovas are incredibly simple to make and great for preparing ahead for a dinner party. Here, the tangy yogurt topping makes a refreshing alternative to the more traditional sweetened heavy cream, and the fresh fruit is juicy and luscious.

6 egg whites

1½ cups caster sugar

1½ teaspoons white wine vinegar

2 pinches of cream of tartar

Topping

5 oz ripe pineapple

1 large ripe mango

2 ripe peaches

1 scant cup 0% fat Greek yogurt

2 teaspoons clear honey

½–1 teaspoon vanilla extract

1 ripe banana

juice of ¼–½ lemon

2 passion fruit

Makes 12

Preparation time: 30 minutes

Cooking time: 45–60 minutes

Chef's Tips

To cube a mango, cut it lengthwise into three, avoiding the central pit. Score the flesh of both pitted sections in a lattice pattern, then push the peel inside out and cut off the cubes.

◆

The pavlovas and yogurt topping can be prepared the day before required and kept in the refrigerator where they will go pleasantly squidgy and chewy. Top with the fruit 1–2 hours before serving.

1   First make the pavlovas. Preheat the oven to 300°F and line a large cookie sheet with non-stick baking parchment. Whisk the egg whites with an electric mixer until stiff, then gradually add the sugar and continue whisking until the meringue is shiny. Whisk in the vinegar and cream of tartar with the last amount of sugar.

2   Mound the meringue in 12 large egg shapes on the baking parchment. Bake for 45–60 minutes until crisp on the outside but still soft inside. Transfer the pavlovas to a wire rack and leave to cool.

3   Make the topping. Peel and pit the fruit as necessary and cut the flesh into small slices or cubes. If the pineapple has a fresh leafy top, reserve a few of the smaller leaves for decoration. Place the fruit in a bowl and stir gently to combine. In a separate bowl, mix together the yogurt, honey, and vanilla extract. Peel and chop the banana and toss in a little lemon juice. Fold into the yogurt.

To Serve   Spoon the yogurt mixture over the pavlovas, then the exotic fruit. Halve the passion fruit and scrape the seeds over the top. Decorate with pineapple leaves, if you have any.

CHILLED FRUIT SOUP WITH BANDOL WINE

On a hot summer's day, chilled seasonal fruits steeped in sweetened wine are very refreshing, and they look sensational in a glass bowl. Serve with a jug of chilled low-fat crème fraîche, and some dainty crisp biscuits if you like.

1 bottle of Bandol wine

⅓ cup sugar

½ lb cherries

¾ lb strawberries

2 white peaches

few drops of lemon juice

1 cup raspberries

finely shredded fresh mint leaves, to serve

Serves 4

Preparation time: 30 minutes, plus chilling time

Chef's Tip

Bandol wine comes from Provence. You can use red or rosé for this recipe, although you are most likely to find the rosé easiest to get. If you can't get Bandol, or you would prefer to use a less expensive wine, you can use any other rosé.

1 Pour the wine into a saucepan. Add the sugar and heat gently, stirring occasionally, until dissolved, then boil without stirring until reduced by half. Pour into a large bowl and leave to cool.

2 Cut the cherries in half and remove the pits. Hull the strawberries and cut them in half lengthwise. Blanch the white peaches in boiling water for 15 seconds, then lift them out with a slotted spoon and peel off the skin. Cut the peaches in half and remove the pits, then slice the flesh.

3 Stir the lemon juice into the cold wine, then add the prepared fruit and the whole raspberries. Cover and chill in the refrigerator for at least 4 hours.

To Serve Transfer to a serving bowl and scatter finely shredded mint over the top. Serve well chilled.

CHAMPAGNE GRANITA

A granita is grainy as its name suggests. Like a water ice or slush, it is cool and very refreshing, just perfect for a hot summer's day. This one is very special, ideal as a dessert at the end of a celebration meal.

⅓ cup sugar

scant cup water

1¾ cups pink champagne

Serves 4

Preparation time: 20 minutes, plus freezing time

1 Put the sugar and water in a heavy saucepan and heat gently, stirring occasionally, until the sugar has dissolved, then boil without stirring until a light sugar syrup is formed (220°F on a sugar thermometer). Remove from the heat and leave to cool.

2 Open the bottle of champagne and pour it into the measuring cup, letting the bubbles subside before measuring it out. Mix the champagne and sugar syrup together, pour into a freezerproof container and freeze overnight until firm.

To Serve Flake the granita into glasses and serve immediately.

Chef's Tip

If you have an ice-cream machine churn the granita in it until frozen, according to the manufacturer's instructions.

◆

Variation

Use a sparkling rosé wine instead of champagne – it is much less expensive.

7

BASIC RECIPES

Y ou can buy light and low-fat basics like dressings and sauces to
keep as a standby, but for freshness and flavor – and to be sure of
what you are eating – there is no substitute for homemade. Take
pasta as an example. Supermarkets and delicatessens have a wide
range of different shapes and flavors labelled 'fresh pasta', but if
you have ever made pasta yourself you will know that commercially
produced fresh pasta is a million miles away from the real thing
made at home. Homemade pasta is so wonderfully light and silky
smooth it hardly needs a sauce.

The recipes in this chapter range from stocks, the foundation of
good home cooking, through to dressings and sauces, vegetables,
pasta, and pancakes. A simple handful of basics with the accent on
fresh, low-fat, and natural ingredients. Some are used in the main
recipe section of the book, others are not, but they are included
here to set you on the right course to healthy eating.

To eat healthily and well, select the best quality ingredients and
cook them with care. If the ingredients are good in the first place,
there is very little need to embellish them. Freshness and simplicity
are the key to successful light cooking.

Chicken stock

This is a basic chicken stock to which you can add flavorings of your choice, such as garlic and fresh herbs. Salt is not used in the making of the stock. It should be added at the time the stock is used.

about 2 lb chopped chicken bones
1 lb mixed onions, leeks, celery, and carrots
1 bouquet garni
8 white peppercorns

1   Place the bones in a stockpot or large, deep saucepan. Finely chop the vegetables and add them to the pan with 10 cups cold water. Bring slowly to a boil, skimming occasionally. Add the bouquet garni. Cover and simmer for 2 hours, adding the peppercorns for the last 5 minutes. Strain through a fine sieve. Allow to cool, then skim the fat from the surface. If not using immediately, cover and chill in the refrigerator. Scrape off any remaining fat on the surface when cold.

◆

Vegetable stock

Mild-flavored vegetable stock is fat-free. If you like, you can use it whenever meat or chicken stock is called for, as a light alternative. The stock is not seasoned when it is made – seasoning should be added when the stock is used in a dish.

1 lb mixed onions, leeks, celery, and carrots
1 bouquet garni

1   Finely chop the mixed vegetables and place them in a stockpot or large, deep saucepan. Add 10 cups cold water and bring slowly to a boil. Add the bouquet garni, lower the heat, and half cover the pan. Simmer gently for 1 hour.

2   Strain through a chinois or other fine sieve, pressing the solids to extract as much stock as possible. If not using immediately, cover and leave to cool, then chill in the refrigerator.

BROWN STOCK

To degrease the stock before using, chill it in the refrigerator overnight. Any fat will solidify on the surface and you will then be able to lift it off easily.

about 2 lb chopped beef or veal bones

1 lb mixed onions, leeks, celery, and carrots

1 scant cup dry white wine or water

1¼ cups chopped tomatoes

2 tablespoons tomato paste

½ cup mushroom trimmings

1 bouquet garni

8–10 black peppercorns

1 Preheat the oven to 425°F. Put the chopped bones in a roasting pan. Finely chop the mixed vegetables and add them to the pan. Roast until browned, about 40 minutes.

2 Transfer the bones and vegetables to a stockpot or a very large, deep saucepan. Degrease and deglaze the roasting pan with the wine or water, then add to the pan with 10 cups cold water. Bring to a boil, skimming occasionally.

3 Roughly chop the tomatoes and add to the pan with the tomato paste, mushroom trimmings and bouquet garni. Cook very gently for 3–6 hours, skimming occasionally. Add the peppercorns towards the end.

4 Strain the stock through a chinois or other fine sieve. If not using immediately, cover and leave to cool, then chill in the refrigerator.

FISH STOCK

Soak the fish bones in a bowl of cold water with a splash of lemon juice for a few minutes, then rinse them well under cold running water. This will get rid of any blood and impurities.

2 tablespoons butter or olive oil

2 cups mixed onion, leek, and celery, finely chopped

1 lb chopped white fish bones

⅓ cup dry white wine

1 bouquet garni

½ cup mushroom trimmings

4 white peppercorns

juice of ¼ lemon

1   Heat the butter or oil in a large saucepan, add the mixed vegetables, and sweat them until softened. Add the chopped fish bones and sweat these for 2–3 minutes.

2   Add the wine and cook until reduced by half, then add 4 cups cold water and bring to a boil. Add the bouquet garni and mushroom trimmings and simmer for 20 minutes, skimming occasionally. Add the peppercorns and lemon juice for the last 5 minutes.

3   Strain the stock through a chinois or other fine sieve. Cover and leave to cool, then keep in the refrigerator if not using immediately. Use within 24 hours.

◆

Chunky tomato sauce

This robust, low-fat sauce is good tossed with pasta, or it can be used in layered vegetable bakes or baked pasta dishes. It can also be served as an accompaniment to broiled or roast poultry and meat. To keep the fat content down, use the sun-dried tomatoes that are sold loose or in packets, not the ones bottled in oil.

1 lb ripe plum tomatoes

¼ cup sun-dried tomatoes

1 x 14 oz can chopped tomatoes

½ teaspoon sugar

2 teaspoons balsamic vinegar

salt and freshly ground black pepper

1   Halve the plum tomatoes lengthwise and remove the cores and seeds. Roughly dice the flesh. Chop the sun-dried tomatoes.

2   Place the sun-dried tomatoes in a saucepan with the canned tomatoes and sugar. Bring to simmering point and simmer for 5 minutes.

3   Add the diced plum tomatoes and cook gently for 10 minutes, stirring occasionally. Remove the pan from the heat, stir in the balsamic vinegar, and season to taste with salt and pepper.

◆

TANGY RED RELISH

Cranberries and orange juice give this relish a sweet and sour flavor, while chilies and coriander give it a spicy kick. It is equally good served warm or cold, as an accompaniment to roast and broiled poultry and meat. It goes especially well with turkey, pork, and venison.

½ teaspoon coriander seeds
2 shallots
1 red bell pepper
2 small red chilies
1 tablespoon olive oil
1 cup fresh or frozen (thawed) cranberries
⅓ cup orange juice
salt and freshly ground black pepper

1 Crush the coriander seeds with a pestle and mortar. Dice the shallots. Halve, core, and deseed the bell pepper and the chilies, then finely dice the flesh.

2 Gently heat the oil in a sauté pan, add the coriander seeds, and fry for a few minutes to release their aroma, stirring all the time. When the seeds are nicely toasted, add the shallots, bell pepper, and chilies. Cook over low heat, stirring frequently, for 5 minutes or until softened.

3 Add the cranberries and orange juice, and add salt and pepper to taste. Stir well to mix, then simmer over moderate heat for about 10 minutes or until the orange juice has evaporated and the cranberries are soft. Serve hot, or cover and leave to cool, then refrigerate and serve chilled.

◆

ROASTED TOMATO DRESSING

This is a basic purée to which you can add more oil or water depending on what you intend to use the dressing for. As it is, it can be spread over chicken or turkey, steaks or chops before broiling. Diluted, it can be used as a sauce.

1 lb ripe plum tomatoes

3 tablespoons olive oil

2 tablespoons fresh thyme leaves

1 tablespoon fresh marjoram leaves

salt and freshly ground black pepper

½–1 teaspoon sugar, to taste (optional)

1   Preheat the oven to 325°F. Halve the tomatoes lengthwise and remove the cores and seeds. Place the tomatoes cut side uppermost in a baking pan and sprinkle with 2 tablespoons of the oil, half the thyme and marjoram leaves, and a little salt and pepper. Make sure that each tomato half gets some herbs and seasoning.

2   Roast the tomatoes in the oven for 1 hour or until they are puckered and shrunken but still moist.

3   Place the roasted tomatoes in a food processor or blender and add 2 tablespoons cold water, the remaining oil, and herbs. Add ½ teaspoon sugar if you think the tomatoes need it. Work until smooth, then taste for seasoning and add more sugar if you like. Turn into a bowl, cover, and keep chilled in the refrigerator until required.

◆

YOGURT AND FRESH HERB DRESSING

Garlic and fresh herbs give this cool and creamy dressing lots of flavor. It is good with potato or cucumber salads, broiled or roast lamb or chicken, or any spicy food.

1 garlic clove

⅓ cup low-fat plain yogurt

3 tablespoons skimmed or semi-skimmed milk

3 tablespoons chopped fresh herbs (eg chervil, flat-leaf parsley, dill)

salt and freshly ground black pepper

1   Finely chop the garlic and place in a screw-top jar with the yogurt, milk, and herbs. Shake until thoroughly mixed, then season generously with salt and pepper.

◆

VINAIGRETTE DRESSING

This is a basic recipe, enough for a salad to serve 4 people. If you like, make a jarful and store it in the refrigerator. It will keep for weeks. Shake the jar thoroughly before use.

2 tablespoons white wine vinegar

1 tablespoon balsamic vinegar

2 tablespoons extra virgin olive oil

1 teaspoon Dijon mustard

½ teaspoon sugar

salt and freshly ground black pepper

1   Place all the ingredients in a screw-top jar and add 2 tablespoons cold water. Shake until thoroughly mixed.

ROASTED RED BELL PEPPER DRESSING

This smoky-flavored dressing goes well with fish and salads, or it can be spread on crackers or crispbreads.

2 red bell peppers
2 tablespoons extra virgin olive oil
6 fresh basil leaves

1   Preheat the broiler. Cut the bell peppers into quarters and remove the cores and seeds. Place the peppers skin-side up on the broiler pan and place under the broiler for 5–8 minutes, or until the skins are blistered and blackened. Place immediately in a plastic bag and allow to cool for at least 10 minutes, or until completely cold.

2   Peel the skin off the bell peppers and place the flesh in a food processor or blender with the oil, basil, 2 tablespoons cold water, and any liquid that has collected in the bag from the bell peppers. Work to a smooth paste.

◆

PASTA DOUGH

Homemade pasta is lighter than bought fresh pasta. This a basic recipe for pasta with eggs (pasta all'uovo) that you can roll out thinly and use to make rectangles or squares for lasagne and cannelloni, or long strips to sandwich together with a filling to make ravioli. It can also be used for long strands such as tagliatelle and tagliarini. These can be made by hand but you will find it easier if you use a mechanical pasta machine. The quantity given here is sufficient for 4 servings.

> 2 cups pasta flour
> 1 teaspoon salt
> large pinch of freshly grated nutmeg or ground mace
> 1 tablespoon olive oil
> 2 eggs
> 1 egg yolk
> flour or semolina, for dusting

1   Mix the flour, salt, and nutmeg or mace in a large bowl. Add the oil, whole eggs, and egg yolk, and mix to form a dough. Turn the dough on to a floured surface and knead for 5–10 minutes until smooth and elastic, adding a little more flour if necessary.

2   Shape the dough into a ball, wrap in cling film, and leave to rest at room temperature for 20 minutes.

3   Roll the dough out thinly, either by hand or machine, and cut into the required shapes.

4   Dust the shapes with flour or semolina and leave to dry on a floured cloth for at least 15 minutes before cooking.

◆

Flavorings for Pasta

Tomato: *Add 1 tablespoon tomato paste with the egg yolks.*

Spinach: *Add 2 tablespoons well-drained cooked spinach with the egg yolks.*

Herb: *Add 2 tablespoons chopped fresh herbs with the egg yolks.*

Saffron: *Add a generous pinch of saffron powder to the dry ingredients.*

MASH

Potatoes that have a floury texture are ideal for fluffy, smooth mash. This recipe is for basic mash. If you like, you can flavor the potatoes with seasonings like freshly grated nutmeg, a few cardamom seeds, or a spoonful of coarsegrain mustard. Crisp, browned onions, scallions, or leeks also make good flavorings. If you are serving the mash with fish, add a little grated lemon rind and juice to the potatoes. This quantity of mash is enough for 4 servings.

3 lb floury potatoes
salt and freshly ground black pepper
¼ cup butter
1 scant cup hot semi-skimmed milk
finely chopped fresh parsley, to serve (optional)

1   Peel the potatoes and cut them into even-size pieces. Put them in a saucepan, cover with cold water, and add 1 teaspoon salt. Bring to a boil and simmer until very tender, 20–30 minutes.

2   Drain the potatoes and return them to the pan. Dry them by shaking the pan over low heat.

3   Mash the potatoes, then add the butter and hot milk, and beat well to mix. Season with salt and pepper. Serve hot, sprinkled with chopped parsley if you like.

◆

CELERIAC PURÉE

Celeriac is a winter vegetable that makes a very tasty purée to serve with meat. It goes especially well with venison and other game. You can serve it in neat mounds or shaped into ovals. This quantity is enough for 3–4 servings.

2 tablespoons butter
2 cups peeled, diced celeriac
salt and freshly ground black pepper
about 4 tablespoons low-fat crème fraîche

1   Melt the butter in a wide shallow pan, add the celeriac, and season with salt and pepper. Cover with a piece of waxed paper and a tightly fitting lid and cook over low heat, testing after 10 minutes to see if it is tender enough to mash with a fork. If necessary, cook uncovered to evaporate excess moisture.

2   Turn the celeriac into in a food processor and purée until smooth, then tip into a saucepan. Warm gently and beat with a wooden spoon, adding enough crème fraîche for the mixture to just hold its shape. Season well with salt and pepper.

◆

THIN EGG PANCAKES

These are oriental-style pancakes that can be used to add protein to stir-fries. Here they are sliced into ribbons, but they can also be left whole and used to wrap around fillings.

2 eggs
salt and freshly ground black pepper
about 1 tablespoon vegetable oil

1   Beat the eggs with ¼ cup cold water and a little salt and pepper. Heat a little oil in a non-stick skillet and add one-quarter of the mixture, tilting the skillet to cover the base with egg. Cook until lightly golden on the underside, about 2–3 minutes. Do not turn the pancake over. Remove the pancake from the skillet and repeat to make 3 more pancakes, adding more oil as necessary.

2   Roll each pancake into a cigarette shape, then cut crosswise with a sharp knife into ¼ inch ribbons.

◆

HERB AND YOGURT PANCAKES

Yogurt, herbs, and Parmesan cheese make these pancakes very tasty and filling. Use them to wrap light vegetable fillings.

1¼ cups all-purpose flour

1½ cups low-fat plain yogurt

1 egg

salt and freshly ground black pepper

2 tablespoons chopped fresh herbs (eg basil, chervil, parsley, marjoram, oregano)

1 tablespoon grated Parmesan cheese

about 6 tablespoons milk

vegetable oil for frying

1   Sift the flour into a bowl. Beat the yogurt and egg together and season well. Add to the flour, stirring until fairly smooth. Add the herbs and Parmesan, and enough milk to thin the mixture down to the consistency of a thick batter.

2   Brush a non-stick 7 inch skillet with a little oil and heat until hot. Drop about 2 tablespoonfuls of the batter into the skillet and spread it out with a palette knife, then cook until bubbles rise to the surface and the underside is golden. Turn the pancake over and cook until the other side is golden, then remove the pancake from the skillet. Repeat with the remaining mixture to make about 8 pancakes altogether, adding more oil as necessary and stacking the pancakes on top of each other as they are done (this will keep them warm).

◆

INDEX